THE MALAY MAGICIAN

The Magician who Dives to Detect a Shoal of Fish

THE
MALAY MAGICIAN

being

SHAMAN, SAIVA AND SUFI

Revised and Enlarged
with a Malay Appendix

by

RICHARD WINSTEDT
K.B.E., C.M.G., F.B.A., D.LITT.(OXON)

KUALA LUMPUR
OXFORD UNIVERSITY PRESS
OXFORD   NEW YORK   MELBOURNE
1982

Oxford University Press
Oxford London Glasgow
New York Toronto Melbourne Auckland
Kuala Lumpur Singapore Hong Kong Tokyo
Delhi Bombay Calcutta Madras Karachi
Nairobi Dar es Salaam Cape Town
and associates in Beirut Berlin
Ibadan Mexico City Nicosia

Revised edition by
Routledge Kegan Paul Ltd., 1951
Further revised and enlarged, 1960/61
Revisions © Richard Winstedt 1961
First issued as an
Oxford in Asia paperback 1982

ISBN 0 19 582529 2

Printed in Malaysia by Sun U Book Co. Sdn. Bhd. Kuala Lumpur
Published by Oxford University Press, 3, Jalan 13/3,
Petaling Jaya, Selangor, Malaysia

CONTENTS

ILLUSTRATIONS

vi

PREFACE

THE aim of this book has been to employ historical and comparative data for unravelling the different elements in a complex system of magic, which scholars working in Europe are apt to summarize as Malay. For the benefit of students of the language I have added in an appendix the Malay original of all spells quoted in the text.

Chronological order is difficult to observe in analysing a system which even in historical time has comprised three elements, pagan, Hindu and Muslim. Hindu influence, for example, has so infected the shaman's *séance* and sacrifice that the chapters on it precede what were parts of Malay magic in prehistoric days. In the last chapter any attempt at chronological order has been abandoned and magic is described as it is applied now to the main problems of life.

Every race has its lumber-room of magical beliefs and practices, and many such survivals are gracious and beautiful and maintain the continuity of a civilization. It is to be hoped that modern materialist ideas will not obliterate them entirely and leave Malay culture jejune.

I am indebted to Dr. Jeanne Cuisinier and the Musée de l'Homme, Paris, for my Frontispiece and Plate I, to Mr. C. A. Gibson-Hill for Plate IV; and for Plate III to Professor Raymond Firth.

This new edition has been further revised especially in the light of Professor M. Eliade's *Le Chamanisme* (Paris). And three new sections have been added to Appendix II.

R. O. W., 1960

I

INTRODUCTION

THIS book deals with the magic of the Federation of Malaya and the magic of Patani, a northern Malay State belonging to Siam. More especially it deals with the magic practised in the Malay States of Kelantan, Perak, Pahang, Selangor and Negri Sembilan. Kelantan was subject to Buddhist Sri Vijaya and later to strong Javanese influence dating back to its conquest by Hindu Majapahit in the fourteenth century; the Perak court is the direct successor of the fifteenth-century court of Malacca, but the state has been influenced by Bugis from Celebes and Minangkabaus from Sumatra; Pahang is an ancient state conquered by Majapahit in the thirteenth century and from the sixteenth has had Minangkabau immigrants; Selangor is Bugis in origin and Negri Sembilan was a colony of mediaeval Malacca, that became swamped by Minangkabaus.

The Malay peninsula is the most southern extremity of the continent of Asia. It has Indochina to the north. South lies the Malay archipelago. It stands midway between India and China. Nature has laid it open to many influences, though Europeans not presented with the evidence of geography, history and religions have been apt to talk as if Malay magic were unique and indigenous.

The language belongs to the Malayo-Polynesian or Oceanic or Austronesian family, which obtained from Formosa to New Zealand and from Madagascar to Easter Island. To the easternmost branch belong the languages of Samoa, Tahiti and Tonga. To the western or so-called

Indonesian branch belong Malay, Malagasy, and languages of the Philippines, Sumatra, Java, Borneo and Celebes. To the Malayo-Polynesian languages are related Khassi in Assam, Munda in central India, Mon in Burma and Siam, Khmer or Cambodian and other languages in Indochina, Nicobarese and the aboriginal languages of Malaya.

Oldest of all the races of the Peninsula are the 3,000 Semang or Pangan of Perak and Kelantan, small, dark, frizzy-haired negritoes, kinsmen of the Aetas of the Philippines and the Mincopies of the Andaman Islands, nomads who in prehistoric times may have left their blood in many of the inhabitants of the Malayan region.

Later aborigines, who build houses and plant rice and millet on the mountains, are the 24,000 wavy-haired cinnamon-coloured Sakai, Indonesians related to many hill tribes in Yunnan, Indochina and the Malay archipelago. A branch of this race, the Besisi, has intermarried freely with the Jakun.

Malaya's 7,000 Jakun are straight-haired, bullet-headed representatives of the proto-Malays, and frequent the forests of Johore and Pahang. In Johore these Indonesians with a Mongoloid strain are known as Orang Benua, 'People of the Country', in Negri Sembilan as Biduanda or followers of the Sultans of mediaeval Malacca, in the modern settlement of Malacca as Mantra and in Selangor as Blanda. The coastal tribes are called Orang Laut or 'Men of the Sea'.

All three aboriginal races show marks of intermarriage and in addition exhibit an Australo-Melanesoid strain due to contact with ancestors of the Australians and Papuans who passed from Indochina down the Malay peninsula some 8,000 years ago.

The civilized or deutero-Malays descended from Yunnan some 4,000 or more years ago, a proto-Malay people who spread over Indochina and thence down the Peninsula to the Malay archipelago, to intermarry during the last 2,000 years with Chinese, Cambodians, Indians, Arabs and all the other foreigners of innumerable small ports.

Before the beginning of the Christian era Indian traders had already visited Malaya, to be followed soon by Brahmins and monks who brought the Hindu religion and Buddhism to its pagan animists. Sanskrit inscriptions attest the presence of Buddhists in Kedah as early as the fourth century A.D. From the eighth to the fourteenth centuries a Malay Buddhist kingdom, Sri Vijaya, dominated the Malacca Straits from Kedah and the northern states, and patrolled the Sunda Straits from Palembang. Then the Thai wrested the north of Malaya from Sri Vijaya, and Hindu Majapahit wrested the south. A rough granite monolith from Trengganu inscribed with Muslim law in a mixture of Sanskrit and Malay and in Arabic script proves the arrival of Islam on the east coast as early as the fourteenth century, and at the beginning of the next century Indians contrived to make it the state religion of Malacca.

A country affected by so many alien influences has had little appeal for the professional anthropologist, who prefers to study the intact customs of primitive tribes. His attitude generally has been that of the Malay who considers that in a perfect state of preservation a neolithic celt has life, but chipped or damaged is dead. This aesthetic liking for the perfect specimen, even of a society, is natural, though if there exists any tribe completely fossilized the study of it would throw no light on the development of the human intelligence, which is one of the prime interests of anthropology.

However, whatever may be the best approach to the study of magic and early religion, the student of the Malay race can exercise no preference. For a people's adaptability to a changing world could hardly be better illustrated than it is by the history of the Malays who during the last 2,000 years have accepted the ideas of two great civilizations, the Hindu and the Muslim, without abandoning their own prehistoric paganism. That paganism can be reconstructed directly from study of backward tribes in Assam, Indochina and the Malay archipelago and, viewed more widely, is of a piece with the paganism of all the races from southern India to China. What has been written of every Dravidian village is true of every Malay village. It is believed to be 'surrounded by evil spirits, who are always on the watch to inflict diseases and misfortunes. . . . They lurk everywhere, on the tops of palmyra trees, in caves and rocks, in ravines and chasms. They fly about in the air, like birds of prey, ready to pounce down upon any unprotected victim. . . . So the poor people turn for protection to the guardian deities of the village, whose function it is to ward off evil spirits and protect the village from epidemics of cholera, smallpox or fever, from cattle disease, failure of crops, childlessness, fires and all the manifold ills that flesh is heir to. . . .' Belief in a vital spirit in all things and the holding of seasonal feasts are common to many races. So is belief in ancestral spirits. But study of the Aetas (Negritos) of Luzon suggests that primitive man in south-east Asia had a god in a Lord.of Beasts, the nomad's food. Then the Negritos of the Andamans and Malaya and the pagan Malay acquired a Sky-God. Belief in a god and even in ancestral spirits demands men skilled in ritual to invoke their aid or placate their wrath.

What is of great interest is the ingenuity shown in the assimilation and reconciliation of old and new beliefs. Often the process was easy. The white blood of Malay royalty, for example, is that ascribed by Buddhists to divinities, by Hindus to Siva and by Muslims to certain saints. Muslim amulets and Sufi mysticism succeeded naturally to the talismans and ascetic practices of Hindus, and those talismans and practices to the fetish and shamanism of primitive days.

INTRODUCTION

But it is startling to find that at a Kelantan *séance* the Malay shaman of to-day still copies Tantric ritual in his opening recital of the story of the creation, in his subsequent worship of gods, and in his concluding asseverance, now in Sufi terms, of man's union with God. For such adaptation of Hindu ritual to Muslim purposes the Malay must have been indebted to the subtle brain of the Indian.

A system of magic that has persisted for thousands of years and borrowed in historic time all that the Hindu and the Muslim could contribute to it must have had practical value. It advocated instead of morality the capricious dictates of the tabu; it asked its gods, even Allah, for no spiritual blessings. It promised no happy after-life, no heaven of bliss. But it was a very present help in trouble. Its ritual gave a sense of order and security to man 'in a world he never made'. Its shamans conjured spirits from heaven to assist the sick and preserve the state, commanding faith by a prestige that went back beyond recorded time and comforting people by the assurance of a hereditary and consecrated priesthood. Even to-day it is the trifling things that console the desperate: the calm voice of a B.B.C. announcer, the promise of a patent medicine, the bedside manner of an indifferent practitioner. The news may be false, the promise of a drug fallacious, the general practitioner incompetent. So, too, the directions that a shaman wrung from the gods might mislead, his herbs and his simples be worthless, his assurance of manner be a veil for hypocrisy. But hope overlooks disillusionment, and the fires of a naïve optimism are never quenched.

Consider the main functions of the Malay magician. He held out the likelihood of rain for crops and of remedies for disease. He taught spells with precise iteration, his insistence that any error in words would mar their cogency enhancing popular respect for their efficacy. He instructed how to sacrifice with such stress on detail as to make men almost

5

forget the risk or disaster that called for the offering. He dealt in charms and philtres that solaced unhappy lovers and brought excitement into dull village lives. He distributed talismans and amulets, that were outward and visible shields against spiritual evil. He was an indefatigable student of 'inaccessible concupiscences and transcendencies' and he whispered to clever neurotic adolescents secrets that fired their minds for abstruse knowledge and disciplined their vague imaginings. He tightened the bonds of communal union by district and state feasts, and so maintained co-operation among rice-planters and fisher-folk. He lifted men out of themselves by traditional rites and ceremonies. Foreign impacts prevented undue conservatism, and in his time and place he held out the promise of science and the aid of religion. He was, in fact, of his primitive society the most indispensable member. For, as Disraeli wrote once, 'Few ideas are correct ones, and what are correct, no one can ascertain; but with words we govern men.'

II

THE PRIMITIVE MAGICIAN

ALTHOUGH the Malay has long been an orthodox Muslim, still in many hamlets there is a Pawang or magician, repository of immemorial superstitions and older faiths. The majority of these traffickers with the supernatural are concerned with fishing and hunting or agriculture or mining and traditional cures for the sick, professing to be expert only in spells and tabus, talismans and amulets and simple methods of divination. A minority practise shamanism, and in an ecstatic trance through a familiar interrogate spirits as to the future or as to the cause and cure of a disease. Temperamentally the two classes differ. The ordinary magician may be a village pundit with his head full of amulets and spells and old herbal remedies; the other like the shaman of Siberia and China starts as a neurotic, a dreamer of dreams and seer of visions. Often the distinction came to be one between hereditary and initiated magicians. In some parts of the Malay archipelago the initiated priest or magician has for his province the cure of the sick and the care of rice-fields and house-building; but only the sky-born hereditary magician (who may also be a chief) can invoke ancestral spirits or act as an intermediary between man and heaven. In Malaya, too, one may search large collections of ordinary incantations in vain for references to Father Sky and Mother Earth and the dead shaman ancestor in tiger form but they always occur in the chants of a shaman at his spirit-raising *séance*, and when they are encountered rarely in the ritual of the rice-field or at the opening of a mine, it may be that a hereditary shaman was

7

officiating or that the old distinction had been forgotten. Even now the shaman is so respected that in Kelantan if he is operating in a district all other medicine-men are disqualified for the time being. However, the development of a settled agricultural society probably encouraged the initiation of many magicians with no hereditary qualification, there being generally no need for a shaman in order to deal with the rice-baby, or teach the appropriate spell for catching a crocodile or the tabus to be observed by collectors of camphor and honey. The two types of magician reflect a differentiation between primitive science and religion. Islam recognized this and the pious Muslim who readily consults the ordinary magician recoils from a spirit-raising *séance* and condemns the shaman as a follower of false gods.

Whatever the origin of the distinction between the two classes, the Malay magician, whether ordinary practitioner or shaman, commands respect by possessing a body of occult knowledge derived often from cultures greater than his own and framed by the ingenuity of many forerunners into an acceptable dogma of superstition. Before he left Yunnan on his southern trek he had got from Babylon or some other centre in the Middle East the practice of divining the future by the inspection of the liver of beasts and by observation of the flight of birds. From the same source, it is surmised, he learnt to employ the incantation or spell[1] and so to have recourse to prayer and sacrifice, if indeed he had not already essayed them.

Incantations presume a belief in spirits, and offerings are

[1] Features of the Babylonian spell that recur in Indian and Malay magic are (1) the ascription of exorcism to some god—'Anu and Antu have commissioned me. . . . Against the might of the sorcerers Marduk lord of incantations has sent me'; (2) the importance of some symbolic act, to which the spell is an accompaniment; (3) the invocation of beneficent gods and spirits against the demons and ills that plague mankind; and (4) an exhaustive enumeration both of benevolent gods and spirits and of demons and evil spirits.

8

an obvious method of propitiating them. Any tree or stone where a community habitually sacrificed tended to become holy and the person who officiated came to partake of its sanctity. If his forebears, too, had been approved intermediaries with the spirits of the countryside, who better than he, their descendant, to ask for harvest and health from his own dead, now after a life's care of the locality resting in its soil? Here was dynasty in the making, if not for the ordinary magician, certainly for the shaman who can communicate with the spirit world and in some regions has been accepted as sky-born or a man-god. Dynasties are commonly credited with a divine origin, and so we find the Mantra declaring Mertang, the first magician, to be the child of the sky-god and the earth goddess. Did these proto-Malays perhaps get this notion too from Babylon, where Marduk, leader of gods and creator of man was priest, looser of tabus and lord of incantations?

Among some at least of the proto-Malay tribes the Batin is both chief and shaman. And it seems likely that differentiation between the Malay chief and shaman is hardly more remote than their conversion to Hinduism. Both hold offices that ideally are hereditary and in any event require some form of consecration; both are masters of an archetypal world; both have insignia baleful to the profane; both have been credited with the possession of familiars and with supernatural ability to injure and to heal and to control the weather; both have been honoured by tree-burial.

In Kelantan a shaman qualified by heredity still ranks higher in popular esteem than one qualified by seeing visions or by study under a teacher. In the same state his consecration, like that of most rulers in Asia and Europe, includes lustration and turning towards the four quarters of the globe. Many countries in the Far East, Japan, Fiji, Timor and others solved the dual functions of leadership by having two sovereigns, one secular, and one spiritual. In the eighteenth century Perak had a state shaman, who was of descent fully royal and bore the title of Sultan Muda or Junior Sultan; at the end of the last century he was a *kramat* brother of Sultan Idris. The holder of this office (which still exists under the title of State Magician) is head of all the magicians in Perak and he is expected to keep alive the sacred weapons of the regalia, to conduct an annual feast and *séance* with libations for the royal drums and to make sacrificial offerings to the genies of the state. Such offerings are still made as part of the ceremony of installing a Sultan of Perak.

Malaysian people as primitive as the Dayaks of Borneo believe that at first the creator of the universe stretched out the heavens no bigger than a mango, and in a Dayak legend a medicine-woman satisfies an army with rice cooked in a pot the size of a chestnut and with meat cooked in a pot the size of a bird's egg. The world of the Malay magician is the breadth of a tray with a sky the breadth of an umbrella. Malay royalty, too, had appanages of the same magical proportions, belonging to that world where Titania's mannikins 'creep into acorn cups' and her fairies 'war with rear-mice for their leathern wings to make her small elves coats'. The shield of the Sultan of that old Sumatran kingdom, Minangkabau, was made of the skin of a louse, his palace pillars of nettle stalks and its threshold-beam from a stem of spinach. A clarionet in the Perak royal band is reputed to be fashioned of the hollow stem of a nettle, and the heads of the Perak royal drums are fabled to be the skins of lice. The same skins covered the heads of drums that belonged to the regalia of the former Raja of Jelebu.

Potent magic attaches to the musical instruments of ruler and shaman. The tambourine of a shaman will generate an evil spirit if not bequeathed to a successor. To tread on a royal drum is to invite death. Even a Chinese has been known to swell up and die after removing a hornet's nest from this terrific instrument.

The Malay shaman (pp. 57-58) and the Malay ruler both own familiar spirits. The familiars of a sultan are the genies who protect his state. In Perak they were supposed to alight on the raja's sword at his installation, even so recent and enlightened a ruler as Sultan Idris wondering if he had not felt a slight vibration. After the annual *séance* and feast to revive the Perak regalia, the state magician would bathe the sultan and in his person those royal familiars, the guardian genies of the country. At a *séance* held during the last illness of another Perak sultan, Yusuf (d. 1887), the royal patient was placed shrouded on the shaman's mat with the shaman's grass-switch in his hand to await, as at an ordinary *séance* the shaman alone awaits, the advent of the spirits invoked. At a famous *séance* held in 1874 to discover if Mr. Birch, the first British Resident, would be wrecked on the bar of the Perak river, Sultan Abdullah himself was a medium and was possessed by nine spirits in succession.

The Malays of the Peninsula often use different names for magicians in general (*pawang*) and those (*bomor*) who practise medicine only, and in Perak and Kelantan different names are given to the ordinary magician (*pawang*) and the shaman (*bĕlian*). Shamanism was the primitive religion of peoples from the Behring Straits to Scandinavia, and spreading to China and Tibet it reached the Malays before they left Yunnan. It is still the sole religion of the Sakai aborigines who entered the Peninsula before them. Among civilized Malays it has survived as a last recourse in sickness or trouble, under a veneer first of Tantric Hinduism and to-day of Sufism. Like his Siberian counterpart the Malay shaman has for his main tasks healing and divination. His familiar speaking through his mouth, he will reveal the name and demands of the spirit causing an epidemic or afflicting a patient with disease so that it can be expelled by the help or advice of a stronger spirit or coaxed out of the sufferer's body either into the shaman's own or usually on to a receptacle that contains an offering of food. Or the shaman falling or pretending to fall into a trance will divulge the whereabouts of lost property, the result of a lover's wooing or of a hunter's chase, or even the fate of a pious pilgrim bound for Mecca!

The existence of the Malay shaman before a nomadic life was abandoned for agriculture is shown by a method reserved down to quite recent times for the disposal of his corpse. That method was exposure upon a branch or in the hollow trunk of a tree or on a platform in a tree or in a hut in the forest. In Timor Laut, in Ceram and among the 'negritoes' of New Guinea the bodies of chiefs are so treated; the negritoes of Kelantan have reserved the noisome honour for magicians. It is an honour that has been paid to them not only by the negrito but by Indonesians like the Sakai of Malaya and the Sea Dayak of Borneo and by the proto-Malay Jakun. A nomadic forest life explains why such exposure has continued to be retained by some wandering tribes for all their dead. But where agriculture led settlers in cleared fields to prefer interment, conservatism was powerless to insist upon the older practice except for the eminent. Two discrepant myths were then invented to explain the survival of a custom originally common and natural. The shaman was exposed in the forest so that he might turn into a were-tiger or so that his tiger familiar might visit him and release his soul or desert his body for that of his successor. (The last shaman to be left unburied in Upper Perak was 'stuck up' in a tree with purple flowers (*Lagerstroemia floribunda*) between 1870 and 1875 and became a tiger with a white patch. Another Perak shaman was interred but scratching his way out appeared as a tiger with one eye closed owing to injury sustained in the grave.) Negritos in Kelantan invented a different myth, namely that exposure in a tree enables the shaman to fly above the head of a fearful figure that blocks the way to the next world. A Jakun myth asserts that the shaman's body is exposed so that his soul may ascend to the sky, a privilege denied to lesser mortals who depart to an underworld. Some Jakun believe that a great shaman is translated alive to the sky. And there are still civilized Malays who hold that the soul of a dying shaman can escape only if a hole is made in the roof. The idea that, unlike common folk, chiefs and magicians ascend to an upper-world occurs with tree-burial among the negritos of the Andamans, and like the idea of a were-tiger is sporadic in the Malay archipelago. The tiger is in fact a dead ancestral shaman who becomes his successor's guide and helps him now in the trance when he is possessed by spirits, as in pre-Hindu days he helped him in the trance when he ascended to heaven. Malaya's negritos reconcile the two myths by saying great shamans communicate with the sky-god and lesser only with the god's son who became a tiger.

War and the acceptance of Hindu and Muslim ideas have led Malays almost invariably to prefer male rulers, but the shaman, product of inspiration as much as of lore, may still be male or, especially in matrilineal communities, female. The female shaman survives among the Mu'ô'ng of Indochina and the Dayaks of Borneo. And when the Malay became Hindu, he found that Trantrism admitted women teachers of its mysteries. Otherwise Indian influence radically altered shamanism. For instead of ascending to heaven in a trance to consult the gods as the shaman of the Far East had always done, the Malay magician now invoked gods and spirits to possess his body, becoming a medium, through whose mouth they spoke.

III

TOWARDS ANIMISM

IT is difficult to write of the primitive mind without ascribing to it theories and systems beyond its reach. Although, for example, the Malay, like many other races, arrived at what has been termed animatism or the idea of a vital force in stone and plant and beast and man, it would be absurd to suggest that he proceeded to postulate uniformity in nature, an idea too abstract for the Malay language even to-day. When again he believed that flagging strength could be restored by contact with objects possessed of abundant vital force, he was merely exercising a puerile logic and drawing a natural inference from the powers of suggestion. It cannot even be claimed that the primitive mind needed any complicated or systematized body of thought to conclude that one might as well entrust an enemy with one's spear or club as put into his power hair or nails which are full of one's vital force. A modern woman instinctively dislikes the idea of another using her nail-file. The savage woman instinctively dreaded the idea of another possessing part of her body, clippings or parings, which malice might knead into a waxen image of her person to be transfixed with pins or melted in fire.

There is another primitive idea which sought to bring the course of nature under human control, and that is the idea of sympathetic or mimetic magic, namely that like produces like, even though the notion may be due to no

more than an impulse to imitate what one desires to happen
and to a natural repugnance to imitate what one dreads
happening. The Malay angler who wants his hook to hold
will almost instinctively keep his teeth clenched. The Malay
gardener who wants fine cobs will plant his maize on a full
stomach and with a thick dibble. Conversely a reaper would
strip herself bare to the waist in order to make the rice
husks thin to pound. Examples are innumerable. If be-
calmed, the Malay sailor would send the ship's cook with
a bowl of rice aloft as high as he could climb, when after
making a great noise he would scatter its contents and invoke a breeze, the bowl being used to symbolize the sky
and the rice representing hail or the pattering drops of
tropical rain. A rice-spoon (which the Torajas of Celebes
dip in water to produce rain) figures in another rain-com-
pelling ceremony from the interior of Pahang. There to
bring down showers before planting out their rice Malays
will wade through the shallows of a river, plant banana-
suckers, sugar-cane and betel and coconut palms on an islet
the drought has created and then to the din of music carry
in procession on the sands a boy or old man arrayed in rain-
calling paraphernalia. His umbrella is a succulent aroid leaf
on whose surface water loves to remain, his cap is the cane-
stand for a cooking-pot and his dagger a rice-spoon. In
many parts of the world a boy or girl is dressed up in leaves
to represent the rich vegetation rain is invited to promote.
The proto-Malay Mantra believe the heavens to be a great
pot suspended over the earth by a string and a common
Malay method of trying to get rain from 'that inverted
bowl we call the sky' is to wash the cooking-pots and their
cane stands. So the Pahang peasant endeavours to procure
the showers he needs by an elaborate symbolic performance.
A plausible explanation of this type of mimetic magic is
that the savage, noting how terrified his neighbour was of
any symbolic design on his person, concluded that the

powers of nature could similarly be intimidated to do his will.[1]

If there are many examples of imitative magic, those of what is often its converse, the tabu, are even more numerous. Where there is a pregnant woman, no old-fashioned Malay will enter by the front door and pass out by the back or contrariwise, because there is one exit only from the womb, the house of life. Neither pregnant wife nor her husband may sit at the top of their house-ladder, as any blocking of a passage protracts delivery. An unplaned house-pillar indented by the pressure of a parasitic creeper that twined round it when it was a living tree will exercise a like obstructive influence. No husband of a pregnant woman should blind a bird or fracture the wing of a fowl for fear his offspring be born sightless or with a deformed arm. If he is an angler, he must not slit the mouth of a fish for fear his child may have a hare-lip. After the engagement of the midwife in the seventh month, the Malay husband (like the Brahmin) may not have his hair cut for fear the afterbirth break. All these may be termed tabus of primitive science as distinct from tabus enjoined to avoid the anger of spirits or a divine king, which are of the nature of religious injunctions.

Oddly enough while it is tabu (*pantang*) to allude to the beauty or health of an infant for fear of inviting the malice of some jealous spirit, there is no ban on mentioning his vitality. 'My goodness, what vitality he has!'—*Wah! semangat*—is a common term of admiration for children. The absence of any ban on its use would appear to be part and parcel of an almost scientific attitude towards vital force considered as impersonal and devoid of individual will, soul or spirit. For the primitive Malay looking below the outer aspect of man and beast and plant and stone found in all of

[1] Mimetic magic and tabu were both supplemented by the spell (pp. 147–150).

16

them an energizing power that permeated them like electricity. It is possessed by all things 'in widest commonalty spread'. There is no 'rank, condition or degree' to distinguish the vital force in man from the vital force in rice or the vital force in an animal. Nor is the idea of immortality associated with it. But certain objects like stones and tough plants and certain parts of the body like the teeth and hair are prized as having it to an abnormal degree. Throughout Indonesia, for example, the *Dracoena terminalis* is a plant, whose indomitable vitality the medicine-man tries to transfer to his patient. The sick are also rubbed with bezoar stones, and a hard candle-nut and a stone are placed both in the cradle of an infant and in the cradle of the rice-baby. The vitality in the hair shorn at a girl's first tonsure is considered so strong that it is buried at the foot of a barren tree to bring fruit as luxuriant as her tresses. In old days, Malay warriors, like Samson, wore their hair long and uncut. Saliva, too, is full of a man's vitality, so that there was a special courtier to guard a royal cuspidore. For everything connected with the body where vital force is present must be protected from the sorcery of enemies, as it was in Egypt and Babylon. A woman's blood can be employed to her hurt by a disappointed lover. Clippings from hair or nails are hidden or destroyed for fear possession of them may give an enemy control over their owner's vital force and endanger his life. This vital force exists even in one's shadow. There is a snail reputed to kill cattle by sucking their shadows. One should not walk upon a person's shadow, and the modern magician to vaunt his power will declare his shadow to be 'the shadow of one beloved by Allah and the Prophet and angels forty and four'.

The imagination of early man, obtruding its fantasies into the province of primitive science associated the idea of vitality with the notion that all objects of the same class have what can only be called external visible souls, generally miniature, of identical form. A cricket is often seen or heard in a Malay house: so in Negri Sembilan the soul of any house is thought to appear as a cricket. The Patani fisherman imagines that even a boat has a soul (*maya Skt.*), generally invisible, to keep it from disintegration: it is lucky to hear the chirping sound of this soul and luckier still to see it. The soul of a dug-out manifests itself as a firefly, that of a large boat as a snake, that of a ship as a person, male or female, according to the quality of the vessel. There is no soul till all the planks have been fitted and the hull can properly be termed a boat. To find the soul of the rattan imagination has no further to go than its mimic, the stick-insect. The soul of the camphor tree, with the romanticism introduced by the Hindu, may appear as a princess or as the cicada she became when her human lover divulged the charms she had taught him, just as the soul of rice may appear as a grasshopper or be adjured as a mannikin to beware of wind and sun and to avoid the bite of sandfly and mosquito. The soul of a man may appear also as that extraordinary phenomenon, the fire-fly. And again, like the soul of eaglewood and the soul of the coconut palm, it is conceived as a bird, so that rice may be sprinkled over a man to retain 'the bird in his bosom' and the soul of the faint be recalled by the same cry that summons chicken.[1]

The flutter of the heart, the vital spark in the fire-fly, the stridulous telegraphy of the cicada in a tree, the rustling

[1] In some parts of the globe it is believed that there are separate souls for the head, the blood, the heart, the saliva and even the foot-prints, and perhaps a survival of this idea is to be traced in the morsels representative of every part of the beast sacrificed which the Malay shaman puts on his altar. A Besisi legend tells of a bright snake with seven souls in the form of iridescent rainbows. The Malay ascribes seven souls to the toddy palm, named after princesses whose 'neck' the tapper seizes, whose blossom-like 'hair' he gathers up and for whose juice he holds an ivory 'bath' where the princesses may 'clap their hands and chase one another'. Respect for the number seven goes back to Babylon but the Malay's romantic address to the toddy palm is likely to be of Indian origin.

flight of a bird from its branches, an uncanny likeness and
the anthropomorphic leanings of men explain the fortuitous origin of these conceptions.

But did the Malay of the Peninsula originally think that
man or beast can be injured by the destruction of this external soul or did he borrow the idea from the Indian? At
the *séance* held in 1874 to discover if the first Resident of
Perak would be wrecked at sea and killed, the Sultan asked
a shaman if he could get Mr. Birch's spirit. The shaman
drew a mannikin figure and hit it with a fan, whereupon
there appeared 'something like a butterfly'. The shaman
killed the butterfly and prophesied the death of the Resident. Negritoes say that butterflies are the souls of Malays
and other foreigners.

The notion of an individual soul can hardly have formed
part of the idea of what was amoral and mortal and took
the same outward visible shape for a whole class of objects.
And the Malay or the Indian missionaries who converted
him to Islam showed a remarkable awareness of the differ-
ence between animation by vital force and the immanence
of soul or spirit in rock, tree or beast. For vital force was
retained the Malay name (*sĕmangat*); to numinous places
and sacred beasts was given the Arabic name, *kramat*. The
passage from rudimentary science to rudimentary religion
is illustrated further by the Malay awe for the strong·per-
sonality of chiefs and magicians, leading to a definite idea
of some kind of personal survival and to the invocation of
the dead to assist the living.[1] What it was that survived
might baffle definition, but it was analogous to the self that
could wander in dreams or, if its tabernacle were a shaman,
be transferred to the body of a were-tiger. And numinous
tree or sacred rock, though lacking the personality of a
nature-spirit, was credited with feelings of dudgeon and
regard that connote an element of reason.

[1] In Polynesia only nobles survive, the souls of common folk perishing
immediately after death.

THE MALAY MAGICIAN

Animism or the idea of a world of spirits the Malay mind seems to have derived from the apparent abundance of vitality in certain persons and objects, and its approach to permanence in solid rock and immemorial tree, in old animals that have dodged the hunter and in men who had so impressed their fellows that for a while at least their personalities appeared to outlast the death of the body.

The magician invokes dead predecessors and chiefs and provides spells against the ghosts of murdered men and of women dying untimely in childbed, ghosts feared by the Malay as by the Dravidian, the Cambodian, the Burman and the Mongol. But no reference is made to the ghosts or souls of ordinary folk except in village verse. One quatrain tells how a girl pats her pillow and calls upon her lover's soul, which comes to her in dreams; in another a lover vows that his soul is caught in the tresses of his sweetheart's hair; in yet another the soul is depicted as weeping in the grave from longing to return to this life. Many pagan tribes in the Malay archipelago believe in individual souls (apart from vital force) that survive after death, and it is possible that the verses cited exhibit traces of a similar belief, long since obliterated first by Hindu ideas of reincarnation and then by the Muslim belief in a resurrection of the dead on a day of judgment. On the other hand, the soul longing to return to life may be only the ghost that according to an old Malay belief haunts the grave for seven days. As a Hindu, the Malay learnt that only the soul of one who has won deliverance is ever entirely separated from the body. But before that, he must have had other ideas of life after death. For the belief of Malaya's aborigines and the Andamanese and many Indonesian tribes in a bridge off which the wicked tumble into an underworld is a survival of a very ancient belief common to central Asia and Siberia (p. 150).

IV

PRIMITIVE GODS, SPIRITS AND GHOSTS

THE primitive Malay mind appears to have conceived spirits of disease formless as vital force, and it invented maleficent auras that emanated from the bodies of murdered men, slain deer, wild pig, wild dogs, certain reptiles and cocks of unusual colour, auras that caused fever or made the hunter blind or mad. In life the bristles on the back of an enraged animal stand on end, and when soon after death they assume the same aggressive attitude, their intention to afflict all within range was easy to infer—and an obvious explanation of the fever that overtakes the trespasser in malarial jungle. Formless, too, appear to have been the gnomes and goblins of the village fields but with a preference for black sacrificial offerings suggestive alike perhaps of their subterranean habitat and of what later, at any rate, was held to be their complexion.[1] For soon the imagination of the Malay came to embody supernatural beings in physical shapes. Father Sky and Mother Earth may have got their human ascriptions from an attempt to explain creation rather than from any definite conception of their form. But anthropomorphism certainly took shape with the worship of dead ancestors, and with belief in the ghosts of youths cut off untimely and of women dying in childbed. There are a few mysterious bachelor spirits like the Black Bachelor and the Boy with

[1] The Malay spirits of the soil appear to have remained male always. In China the Han period (140–87 B.C.) saw male local spirits of the earth give way to a cosmic earth goddess. The advent of the Hindu anticipated such a change among the Malays and Siva became the cosmic earth-god with Sri as the goddess of agriculture.

the Long Lock of Hair, of whom Perak peasants speak, or the Bachelor Cockfighter who presided over mains and hates liars. There is a banshee (*Langsuyar*), generated by the malevolence of a woman dying in childbed, which can wear the form of a beautiful girl, whose flowing tresses rustle like rain as she flies in the dark to alight on a tall tree or hide in the bird's nest fern. The revengeful ghosts of such young mothers and of murdered men are driven away by charms and amulets, prickly thorns, ashes and the stench of burnt herbs. But to the benevolent spirits of chiefs, founders of settlements and magicians the homage of incense is offered. At a *séance*, for example, the incantations will include supplications to dead magicians, the ancestors of the medium. In Upper Perak a feast (p. 66) to the spirits of the district was accompanied by invocations addressed to bygone magicians and to a raja who opened the territory. A Malay ruler, too, looks to his ancestors for the protection of his person and his State, visits their scattered tombs after his installation or before any great enterprise, and, if sickness afflicts a member of the royal house, sets a cooling potion for the patient overnight upon an ancestral grave. The graves of magicians have also been the resort of suppliants, who risk tribulation if they neglect to sacrifice the goat or cock vowed for the fulfilment of their requests. Such graves, many of them under great trees, are often guarded by were-tigers and a few by crocodiles. None of these benevolent spirits of the dead are homeless ghosts: they are attached to a place or a clan. There is a chief of Mt. Berembun in Perak and there is Dato' Paroï, lord of Gunong Angsi in Negri Sembilan, who commands a ghostly crowd that come out of their graves as were-tigers. A were-tiger guards even the Fairy Princess of Mt. Ophir, who reclines in a cave, a beautiful girl on a couch of dead men's bones. Some relate how every morning she appears as a girl, every noon as a woman, every night as an old beldam.

One legend tells how in the guise of a hag carrying a cat and a bag of saffron, she will ask boatmen on the Gemencheh river for a lift; if it is refused, the boat runs aground; as soon as she is taken aboard, it glides off. When she leaves the boat, she gives each man a piece of saffron that turns to gold in his hand. The bag and the gold suggest a late origin for this fairy. But even if we stick to primitive ancestral spirits, there is no convincing evidence that their worship is the oldest of Malay religious practices. For ancestors are invoked to aid in propitiating spirits of soil and sea and river who are already in existence.

A human shape once conceived for apparitions, fancy invented an army of anthropomorphic spirits and fairies who had no connection with ancestors.

There is a mysterious Grannie Kemang (perhaps the Tibetian Khŏn-ma, chief of earth demons), who is known to the proto-Malay Mantra and to the civilized Malays of the Peninsula and of Sumatra. The Mantra say that she lives in the ground and causes swellings of the hands and feet. In Perak it is thought that she will sow tares, a refuge for goblin pests, on the fresh clearing, unless the farmer rise betimes to alleviate with cool offering the smart of the burnt forest.[1]

There is the Spirit that Undoes Snares (*Hantu Sungkai*), invisible below the breast, with an enormous nose and wide-slit eyes that see all about him.

There is Ma' Kopek, a hag that causes nightmare. Children playing hide-and-seek may lose themselves behind her prodigious breasts and be found days later dazed and foolish. Sometimes she will decoy them to a thorn-brake and

[1] There are other and probably later and less authentic Perak legends. One credits Grannie Kemang with giving two slave girls the tiny reaping knife used by Malays not to frighten the rice-soul and instructing them how to cultivate that cereal. Yet another legend makes her the embodiment of the rice-soul. And her cooking-pot is regarded as the inexhaustible cruse of the Malay peasant.

feed them on earth-worms and muddy water, changed by her magic to look and taste like delicious cakes.

There is a grey dishevelled Kitchen Hag, who warms herself before the hearth at night and loves to blow into flame the embers in a deserted house.

Nature-spirits, too, assume some of them a human shape. There are bright-eyed echo-spirits like men and women in stature, who entice the lonely woodcutter to palaces invisible to other eyes. Those who return bring back fairy gifts, silks and cloths that turn alas! to leaves. If an echo-spirit visits a mortal woman, she will bear an albino child. A Kinta Malay once married one who in three weeks gave birth to an infant no mortal could suckle.

Spirits like these are shapes from the nursery of mankind. But like the hysterical patient to-day, so the neurotic Malay shaman could body forth animal monsters as various as the creations of Hieronymus Bosch. There is a scaly ginger-coloured prodigy (*Balun Bidai*), rectangular and like a mat with a mouth at every corner: it lives in pools and enwraps man or boat, drowning its prey and sucking all the blood out of a body without causing a wound. There is the Puaka, a pig-like spirit that also inhabits river-pools. Then in Perak when choosing a place for a woman's delivery, the magician has to beware of soil likely to be haunted by a Kertau, a goblin with the body of a boar and the antlered head of a deer. Another prodigy is the Spook that Drags Himself Along, in the shape of an orang-outang; he will peep into attics where fair maids sleep, and once he carried a girl off up a tree and lived with her as his wife. Throughout Malaysia terror is felt at the cry of the Pontianak, a banshee in the form of a bird that drives her long claws into the belly of an expectant mother, killing her and her child. That other banshee, the *Langsuyar*, may assume either the shape of a beautiful girl with a hole in the nape of her neck or the shape of an owl with the face of a cat. To prevent a woman dying in childbed from becoming either of these banshees, glass beads are put in the corpse's mouth to keep her from inhuman shrieking, hen's eggs laid under her armpits so that she will not lift them to fly, and needles placed in the palms of her hands so that she may not open or clench them to assist her flight. Another spirit that sucks with fatal result the blood of an expectant mother is the *Penanggalan*, a woman's head and neck with trailing viscera.

Finally there is a class of familiar spirits created from the dead. Some Malays say that their several names are only dialect terms for one familiar, but others distinguish three types, the *Bajang*, the *Polong* and the *Pělěsit*; yet others exclude the *Bajang* as a malignant forest spirit.

As a familiar, the *Bajang* may be the hereditary property of his owner, but more often is conjured at night from the newly dug grave of a stillborn child. He is kept in a stoppered bamboo vessel and fed with eggs and milk; released, he will cause sickness and delirium to his victims, especially children. Formerly in Perak anyone discovered by a magician to be keeping a *Bajang* was generally put to death.

Then there is the *Polong*. Pour the blood of a murdered man into a bottle and recite the appropriate incantation, and after seven, or twice seven, days a bird-like chirp will announce its presence. Every day the owner of this familiar must feed it with blood from his or her finger. Its victim will die raving, unless through his mouth the *Polong* confess the name of its owner and that of any malicious person who may have hired it from that owner.

The best known of all these familiars is one (*Pělěsit*) of the nigget type. A woman goes into the forest on the night before a full moon, and standing with her back to the moon and her face confronting an anthill she recites certain incantations and tries to catch her own shadow. It may take three nights. Or she may have to try for several months, always on the same three nights. Sooner or later she will succeed and her body never again cast a shadow. Then in the night a child will appear before her and put out its tongue. She must seize the tongue, whereupon the body of the child vanishes. According to a more gruesome version the tongue must be bitten out of the corpse of the first-born child of a first-born mother exhumed from a cross-roads grave. However got, the tongue will turn into a tiny animal, reptile or insect, which has to be fed on eggs or on blood from its owner's finger. A favourite shape for this familiar is that of a house-cricket. This vampire cricket is employed especially by jealous wives to injure a rival or that rival's children. It enters the victim's body through the ear, and if mastered by a medicine-man quits it by way of the fontanel. The method of its acquisition was practised by Malaya's aborigines and in Indochina.

Although for some fifteen hundred years the Malay has been subject to the influence of two great historic faiths, even to-day these local goblins and gnomes, ghosts, banshees and familiars mean far more to him than the cosmic gods and demons of the Hindu, or the Arabian genies of Islam. Although in Hindu times their places were usurped by Siva and by Sri the goddess of agriculture, still in the ritual of the rice-field, at a Kelantan *séance* and at the openings of mines and theatrical shows Father Sky and Mother Earth are invoked by the shaman as beneficent powers. Ancestral spirits he also invokes for their kindly disposition to man. And if banshees and familiars are always malignant, yet nature-spirits in spite of caprice can be benign. For the bite of a water-snake a Malay will invoke the water-spirit and sprinkle water over the wound. And a hunter dizzy from the revengeful aura of a slain animal will smear his person with mud and clay, thus putting himself under the protection of the local earth-spirit just as a Greek actor put himself under the protection of the god of wine by smearing his face with wine lees.

V

HINDU INFLUENCE

INDIAN traders reached Malaya at the very beginning of the Christian era. Inscriptions and images testify to the presence of Buddhists in Kedah and Perak by the fourth and fifth centuries A.D. Next, Pallavas from the Coromandel coast founded Hindu settlements in Kedah. Then Mahayana Buddhists from the Pala kingdom of Bengal came and there are traces of the Tantrism that attempted to reconcile Buddhism with the worship of Siva. From the eighth century onwards the north of Malaya was under the Malay Buddhist kingdom of Sri Vijaya. In the fourteenth century its colonies in Malaya were conquered by Hindu Majapahit. There are, it is true, Buddhist traces in Malay magic and ritual, like the use of rice-paste in place of oil for anointing. But the evidence goes to show that Hinduism was as predominant in Malaya as in Champa where out of 128 inscriptions only seven are Buddhist and ninety-two Sivaite.

Between the primitive beliefs and practices of the Malay and those of the Hindu there was much in common. In Vedic times heaven and earth, rivers and mountains and plants were supplicated as divine powers, and drums and weapons were regarded as potent fetishes. In the *Atharvaveda* (600 B.C.) will be found belief in the efficacy of piercing a mannikin figure to harm an enemy as well as the ancient rite of anointing kings and the original of a Malay love spell extant to-day. As by the Malays so by Indians, the Babylonian incantation, Babylonian divination, the Babylonian belief in witchcraft and in evil spirits have been too assimilated for close definition.

27

The greatest gifts the Indians brought to the Malay race were a vocabulary of abstract terms like *religion, asceticism, fasting, teacher, incantation,* an alphabet, the conception of a state and a god-king, profound respect for teachers and learning, and cosmic deities to control local spirits. Indian influence lasting a thousand years affected every department of magic.

Hinduism in Tantric form fortified the Malay shaman by corroborating the efficacy of fasting and seclusion and confirming the notion that trances bring supernatural power. It taught him a Sanskrit term (*tapa*) for 'ecstatic fervour' and the meditation that makes a great magician. It prepared him for his later visions as a Sufi mystic by teaching him to quell desire by meditation on corpses till the world appears full of skeletons. It instructed him how to absent himself from this spatial universe by counting the inhalations and exhalations of his breath and concentrating his gaze on his navel. He was told how before losing consciousness and gaining deliverance from the cycle of existence with power to transport himself anywhere at will the ascetic 'hears within his body (in the heart and throat and between the eyebrows) various sounds, those of a drum, the roaring sea, thunder, a bell, a reed, a lyre, a shell or a bee'. As a Muslim, the Malay often claimed the power to transport himself anywhere at will. It was said of an eighteenth-century ruler of Perak that every Friday he would visit Mecca and once brought back three green figs as proof of his journey. On the beach at Singapore is the sacred grave of another Malay, a humble clerk, Habib Noh, who was credited with the same supernatural power. Although it was as a Hindu that the Malay first became acquainted with this department of magic, yet while still a pagan animist he had valued the ecstatic trance, believing like William Blake that 'the path of excess leads to the palace of wisdom'.

Whether ascending to heaven in a trance or in the ordin-

ary practice of his calling, the primitive Malay magician
had attempted already to control the spirits with which he
trafficked, by the incantation. The voice of the animist is
heard in the invocation calling the corn-baby to her cradle
or in the sailor's call for a breeze: 'Come, wind, loose
your long flowing tresses,' or in the Perak raftsman's address to the spirit of a perilous rapid: 'Accept this offering,
grandsire. Send our raft safe through the long rapid, we
beseech thee! Cause us no harm on our journey. Open like
the uncurling blossom of the palm! Open like a snake that
uncoils.'

The incantation even of the pagan Malay shaman was not
diffident like these entreaties by rice-planter and boatman.
And now his confidence was reinforced by the assurance of
the Brahmin, and his repertory immensely enlarged from a
written source. For instance. An incantation used by the
Malay when tin-ore has been reached in a mine follows
exactly the Indian myth of the creation in the *Satapatha
Brahmana*, namely that in the beginning was created water,
then foam, then earth. The Malay incantation declares how

From dew there came water,
From water there came foam,
From foam there came earth,
From earth there came ore.

And even to-day Malay invocations bear all the characteristics of the Indian *mantra*. They should be kept secret.
They are in rude metrical form. Many are a mixture of
prayer and spell. Many, too, for the cure of sickness or the
control of epidemics or the cleansing of a state from spirits
inimical to fecundity of soil and beast, became part of elaborate rituals accompanied by sacrifice that to the mind of
the Hindu daily recreates the world. In Kelantan the *mantra*
used at these rituals are Tantric in their order, beginning
with a recital of the story of the creation, then invoking the

gods and concluding with the modes of union between God and man.

In a charm to weaken a rival the Malay copying the arrogance of the Brahmin will boast

> *It is not on the earth that I tread!*
> *I tread on the heads of all living things!*

To frighten and capture a male tiger he will, like the Brahmin, stand on one leg at sunrise and vaunt his powers:

> *My countenance is the light of breaking day!*
> *My eyes are the stars of dawn!*
> *My body is that of a tusker!*
> *My prop is a fierce tiger!*
> *My seat is a ravening crocodile.*

Sitting on the skin of a tiger was supposed by Hindus to give invincible strength.

Under Indian tutelage the Malay also learnt an alphabet and was initiated into the efficacy of words of power like the mystic Om, which symbolizes the Hindu triad, Visnu, Siva and Brahma. As late as 1880 in Perak it was considered so awful that reading aloud three times elephant charms in which it appeared was thought certain to stop all the hens in the neighbourhood from laying. For the Malay still recited it even after he had become a Muslim, and he confused the tiger (once an avatar of Siva) with 'Ali, the Prophet's son-in-law.

> *Om! Virgin goddess Mahadevi! Om!*
> *Cub am I of mighty tiger!*
> *'Ali's line through me descends!*
> *My voice is the rumble of thunder,*
> *Whose bolts strike a path for my seeing!*
> *Forked lightning's the flash of my weapons!*
> *I move not till earth rocks!*

HINDU INFLUENCE

I quake not till earth quakes,
Firm set as earth's axis.

That is a charm against a thunderstorm. Mahadevi, the
wife of Siva is invoked because under this new Hindu influence beast and spirit are adjured in terms of a new
religion and a new mythology:—

> *Obey my words, trapped elephant.*
> *If thou obeyest not,*
> *Thou wilt be killed by Sri Rama;*
> *If thou obeyest,*
> *The great Rishis will keep thee alive.*

Or take a spell against smallpox:

> *This is not my spell!*
> *It is the spell of Narada;*
> *It is the spell of Samba.*

That Hindu incantations came to be part and parcel of
Malay sacrificial ritual can be seen in Kelantan where a
Sanskrit term *puja* is still known as the name for the ancient
rite of 'cleansing' the state. And though the pyramidal altar
used by the Malay for great sacrifices was perhaps borrowed
from Babylon, now that the offerings laid upon it were for
Hindu *dewa*, it was given a Sanskrit name (*panca prasada*)
and in Perak its summit was crowned by an image of Jatayu, offspring of Visnu's Garuda. Wang Ta-Yuan reported
human sacrifice in Trengganu in 1349 before images of
fragrant wood apparently by Tantric worshippers of Kali,
the dread Hindu goddess of death, and Fei Hsin claims to
have seen it in Pahang in 1436. In Kelantan an invocation
at a state *seance* still calls upon Siva as Kala the Destroyer.

The sacrifice at a state function bears traces of ritual introduced by the Sivaite Brahmins, who were about a
Malay court in former days. But the books of magicians

31

still contain directions for many humbler occasions when the Hindu Malay made offerings to Siva. The hunter who had snared a deer was to wrap in a leaf portions of her eyes, ears, mouth, nose, feet, liver, heart and spleen and put the packet in the slot of his victim as a present for the Hindu god. The man who had lost property had to make a small offering to Siva and implore his help to recover what had been lost. The actor about to open his travelling theatre still presents an offering with a prayer to the blue-throated Siva and to all the gods of the Ramayana to protect his troupe from illness and poverty. For though the Malay has been a Muslim for five hundred years, such Hindu ritual has been tolerated down to modern times under the convenient fiction that Siva is chief of the infidel genies subservient to Allah.

India also brought the Malay systems for taking omens more sophisticated than the Babylonian inspection of livers and inferences from the flight of birds. The day was now divided into five times (*kutika Skt.*) named after Maheswara (Siva), Kala the Destroyer, Sri the wife of Visnu and guardian of agriculture, Brahma and Visnu. A cycle of five days assigned to the same Hindu deities in the same order was also introduced. At any time sacred to Maheswara, the Malay was instructed, one meets fair people, profits from deals in white goods, recovers any slave who absconds eastwards and wins a main with a white cock. Under Kala one meets rogues, finds it hard to recapture any slave who has absconded downstream, receives bad news, must sacrifice a black cock to cure illness and use a black cock to win a main. Under Sri one must enter a white cock to win, sacrifice a red and white cock for the sick, and may expect to recover any slave who absconds westward. Brahma's colour is red, and at any time sacred to him the slave who flees westward will escape. The colour of Visnu is green. At times sacred to him the traveller will encounter floods or

THE MASTER OF A SHADOW-PLAY CENSING AN OFFERING

[To face p. 32

rain, and if invited into a house, will be given green vegetables; if one sails, one will be upset or encounter storms; a
slave fleeing southwards will be captured under a green tree
near a river. This type of prediction is extremely old. The
mythical Greek poet, Melampus, forecast days of the month
propitious for recovery from illness and for the purchase
and recapture of slaves.

The Malay's acquaintance with Hindu astrology is shown
in the political constitution of mediaeval Malacca and of the
modern states of Perak, Negri Sembilan and Pahang as well
as Burma, Siam, Cambodia and Java, where for the luck of
the kingdoms the greatest dignitaries were four, the lesser
eight and sixteen and the lowest thirty-two in number.
Even the pillars of an old Perak palace numbered four sets
of eight, totalling thirty-two. 'A passage of the New History in the Tang dynasty,' Dr. von Heine-Geldern reminds
us, 'indicates that the kingdom of Java in the ninth century
was divided into twenty-eight provinces, corresponding to
constellations, the twenty-eight Houses of the Moon, and
the four Ministers to the guardian gods of the cardinal
points. It is clear that in all these cases the kingdom was
conceived as an image of the heavenly world of stars and
gods.' For plus the king the number thirty-two made up
the number of gods on Mount Meru, the heaven of Indra.
And the Malay god-king introduced from India to cure men
of sickness and secure fertility for crops and herds often
took the title of Indra (master magician and lord of weather)
and had hill, temple or palace symbolizing Indra's Hindu
Olympus. At Sri Menanti in Negri Sembilan the hill behind the palace is still called the Mount of Holy Indra.

The Hindu stations of the moon were responsible for the
twenty-eight rĕjang, into which the lunar month of the
Malay was divided, each of them distinguished by a symbol, usually an animal. As with the Hindu, the symbol of
the first station is a horse, though after that the Indian and

33

Malay symbols differ. Each of the stations is lucky or un-lucky for planting, travelling, weddings, illness and the recovery of stolen property. To neutralize a bad omen, one throws away on the first day an image of a horse towards the east and so, too, the symbol of any other unlucky day.

The lore of the ascetic and the intricacies of astrology can have had little attraction for the ordinary man and even the myths of the Hindu gods commanded popular interest only on the screen of the shadow-play. But for the magician who must know the origin and temper of every god and spirit he would invoke, Hindu mythology was of incalculable importance. He had to know that Batara Guru, the Lord Teacher, as Malays call Siva, was at once the white spirit of the sun and the black spirit of the earth. Siva could assume a thousand shapes, but unlike the local spirits under his command he was a cosmic deity. He was Mahadeva, the Great God. He was Nataraja, lord of dancers and king of actors, whose theatre is the world and himself actor and audience. Identical with Rudra, storm-god and leader of lost souls, Siva was also the Spectre Huntsman or Raja of Ghosts, whose passing in the tempest would keep the Malay peasant silent from awe. And like the Bhils, Kols and Gonds of India, so too the Malay discovered in Siva Gaffer Long Claws, the tiger, oldest familiar of his shamans. Under the name of Sambhu, the Auspicious, he discovered in him also an avatar of the crocodile, lord of the water as the tiger was lord of the jungle. Above all, wherever Siva was wor-shipped, he was Kala the Destroyer with the necklace of skulls and as Kala he was also the black god of the devouring sea.

The magician knew, too, that Kumari, the Virgin, and Mahadevi, Great Goddess, and Kali or Durga, Goddess of Death, are all descriptions of the consort of Siva. But more important to a rice-eating race was Sri, the Hindu and Malay Ceres, actually the wife of Visnu but frequently

mistaken by the Malay for a consort of Siva. Siva, Berma
Sakti (or Brahma), Visnu and Krisna are often invoked
together to protect the peasant clearing land for rice-planting. The magician will vaunt that the sword of Visnu is
before his face to protect him and in Kelantan he invokes
Krisna to cure the bite of snakes and the sting of centipedes
and scorpions.

Of lesser Hindu demons and demi-gods the Malay
magician has the vaguest knowledge. The Asuras, exalted
demons that war not against men but gods, are represented
by Rahu, who causes eclipses of the sun and moon and to
the Malay mind is a huge dragon. Danu, a demon relation
of his in Hindu mythology, is the serpent who inhabits the
rainbow. In the north, where plays founded on the Ramayana are popular, Sri Rama, the hero of that epic, is a
demi-god invoked especially by elephant-hunters, and
Hanuman the monkey-god is an evil spirit. There, too, the
Rishis or great sages are invoked, and the magician takes
refuge (p. 31) behind the name of the sage Narada and the
name of Samba, a son of Krisna, who mocked Narada and
his companions.

Acquaintance with Bhuta and Raksasa is due mainly to
popular romances borrowed from the Deccan. The Malay
will turn, for instance, to the story of Marakarma (or Si-
Miskin) and read of a Raksasa who lights a fire as big as a
burning town, pours rice on a mat a hundred yards wide
and eats it along with spiders, centipedes, lizards, flies and
rats that overcome by the steam drop on to his food; who
drinks a well of water, hiccups like thunder, and picks from
his teeth with a log chunks of food so large that they kill
cat, goose or fowl by their impact.

Indian magic made itself felt not only in the Malay
séance, the sacrifice and divination but in the political and
domestic life of the Malay. In the political sphere it introduced the idea of a god-king, bringing thus to fruition the

half-unconscious dream of the pagan Malay and for ever relegating the Malay magician to a subordinate place in society. The shaman was the receptacle of a god only for a brief while during his *séance*: the new king was the receptacle of a god for life. The shaman communicated with heaven only during his *séance*. The god-king was permanently associated with light; he wore yellow garments, the colour of the sun, and albinos whether bird, beast or child were his perquisites. His touch could cure, and the humour of his body controlled the weather and made rice-fields fertile.

Like the shaman, however, a king had to be consecrated to obtain his virtue. And his consecration involved a magical ritual with details of immemorial antiquity. The old common man was washed clean. After that lustration, the new man was anointed, not with oil like a Hindu god but with the rice-paste which Buddhism substituted for it in Malaya, Siam and Cambodia. The significance of details forgotten, lustration and anointing are now apt to be merged. In Negri Sembilan, for example, the Ruler, sitting on a nine-tiered *bathing* pyramid, dips his right hand four times into bowls of rice-paste proffered for his anointing by four court officials. Not only has sitting on a bathing pyramid taken the place of lustration but there is another point in the original symbolism that has been forgotten. In Siam after lustration the king dons royal dress and turns about on his throne to receive conches for anointment, one at each cardinal point; in Negri Sembilan the fourfold anointment in one position is a mere shadow of the older cosmic symbolism. Again, in Vedic times an Indian king was given at his enthronement a wooden sword termed a thunderbolt as a weapon against demons. To-day in the head-dress of a Perak Sultan is thrust a mediaeval seal, whose handle is reputed to be made of thunder (*gĕmpita* Skt. corrupted *kampit*) wood that 'causes matter to fly': it is called the lightning seal (*chap halilintar*) and must have taken the place of Indra's *vajra* or thunderbolt, so often depicted in Javanese sculpture. Royally clad, the Malay ruler is next taken in procession round his capital or demesne the way of the sun, and this procession round the capital, hill or palace that stood for Mt. Meru is in fact a symbolic taking possession of the kingdom. Next, the new ruler is conducted to his throne to sit there with the immobility that in Hindu ritual is the evidence of incipient godhead. And now just as a Brahmin whispers into the ear of his pupil the name of the god who is to be the child's protector through life, so in Perak the chief herald, descended from the vomit of Siva's bull, Nandi, whispers into the ear of his master the state secret, namely the title of the original ancestor of the royal house. In Negri Sembilan the election of the new Yang di-pertuan is announced by the Herald on the Right in Brahminical attitude, that is, standing on one leg with the sole of the right foot resting against the left knee, his right hand shading his eyes and the tip of the fingers of his left hand pressing his left cheek. And just as in Vedic ritual the guardians of five regions of the sky were invoked, so in Negri Sembilan one of the four court officials with a Sanskrit title implores the blessing and protection of five angels of the sky and again of the horned angel of the moon and the four archangels of Islam; the regalia are displayed and a copy of the Kuran is set down before them and before ewers of water mixed one with blood, another with rice-paste and another containing a bullet. In Perak (and Siam) newly appointed chiefs used to be sworn to allegiance by drinking water in which the state sword had been dipped. Elevated into the ritual of a religion, nearly every detail of these Hindu court ceremonies is magical in origin.

When we come to domestic magic, there is little Hindu influence on birth ceremonies except a rite in the seventh month of pregnancy and perhaps the introduction of the child to Mother Earth and Father Water. Nor again has Hindu cremation survived for the dead. But on the ceremonial side Malay marriage (pp. 116–122) has remained completely Hindu. For pagan Malays, with their trial intimacies for adolescents, the final selection of a wife may have been no great occasion. For the Hindu a bride and groom were prince and princess on the auspicious day of marriage, and the Malay dropping his pagan nonchalance welcomed this novel attitude with the eagerness that has always characterized his experiments for the exaltation of man. For that exaltation Hindu courts brought him the pomp and ceremony which have remained the pride of his race.

Finally India introduced to the Malay a new stock of talismans. As a pagan he prized every object with strong vital force: stones, candle-nuts, cockle-shells, hardy grass that survives the traffic of a road, a strange knot in a Malacca cane, an unusual whorl on the wooden sheath of a creese, an accidental mark in its damascene, all these commanded his awe and trust. So did those wonderful things, instruments of music. The musical instruments and the collection of oddments, glass balls, weapons and so on, that had come into contact with a line of chiefs were also powerful talismans from pagan times, so that even as late as 1896 when the Perak war caused the removal of that state's regalia to Singapore the peasants ascribed to their absence bad harvests and diseases among their cattle. But the Malay was always on the look out for fresh magic, and India brought new weapons for his spiritual armoury, tinsel crowns to protect bride and groom, a protective thread to tie round the wrist, incense to scare demons, the waving of holy water over the sick and the newly married, and perhaps the rubbing of the frail and the ill and those in ghostly peril with yellow turmeric, red betel and black ashes.

VI

THE RITUAL OF THE RICE-FIELD

IN the ritual of the rice-field survive magical practices that may well go back to the emergence of the Malay as an agriculturist. Strip away the obvious accretions, the names of Hindu deities, the thin Muslim veneer, and the essence of the ritual remains intact in Malaya to-day. It deals with soul-substance, human, animal, vegetable, with the spirits of dead magicians, nature-spirits and Father Sky and Mother Earth. Except for Sky and Earth the spirits invoked lack the omnipresence and individuality of gods, bear generic names and are indefinite in number. Their sphere is a particular district. They inhabit the rice-field, the thick jungle, the rays of the setting sun. No temples are erected in their honour. The customary and symbolic rites that persuade them to friendly relations with man can be enacted in a forest clearing, in the corner of a rice swamp, on the floor of a village barn. The magician has the narrow scope of the spirits he serves. He belongs to one small village or humble district. He may even call upon an old Malay midwife to plant the first seedlings so as to make a crop prolific. Among many aborigines the rites are celebrated not by a man but by a woman, fitting midwife for the rice-baby.

First of all there may be a ceremony that has been traced back to ancient China as a spring festival of youth connected with rain-making, and is now conducted by the Malays of Selangor and Negri Sembilan to expel evil spirits before clearing their fields for planting. Of this festival in an earlier stage there is an account in the fifteenth-

century Malay version of the Javanese romance entitled
Chekel Waneng-Pati. Princes and princesses with their
followers pick flowers (perhaps to ward off evil influences),
visit ancestral sites, sing antiphonal songs, celebrate weddings and witness a mock combat in which youths of
different provinces hurl calladium stems at one another.
Nowadays every three or four years the Minangkabau
Malays of Negri Sembilan enact a spring ceremony that
lasts seven days with a similar mock combat. Sometimes
banana stems are the weapons. Sometimes the two oppos-
ing parties hurl across a gully thin rods with pared flat ends
(like that of an old-fashioned stethoscope) until a blow
makes the face of one of the combatants bleed and ends
the fray. Sometimes even stones are the missiles. Apparently
in ancient China (as in Abyssinia) blood-letting by combat
was a homoeopathic way of compelling rain, and Javanese
rice-planters will thrash one another, till blood flows, for
the same end. To-day, as the accompanying incantations
prove, the combat is explained by Malays as a fight against
evil spirits, and though this interpretation is difficult to reconcile with the two teams of human combatants, it recalls
a spring expulsion of devils in Tonquin, Cambodia and
Bali. There is no record of it from Kelantan or Perak, where
the expulsion of spirits by river (p. 168) may take its place.
In Negri Sembilan it is common, and there a pink buffalo
will be slaughtered upstream for spirits and downstream a
black one, portions of whose blood and flesh are distributed
to participants to bury in their fields as offerings to earth-
spirits. The magician opens proceedings with an adjuration
too full of Muslim lore to be old:

> *In the name of Allah, the Merciful, the Compassionate!*
> *Ancestors that inhabit the layers of the earth!*
> *Genies of the soil! Idols of iron!*
> *Get ye aside, genies and devils!*

THE RITUAL OF THE RICE-FIELD

Make way for the might of Allah.
You who thrust up to peer
Bow down, for as a tiger I pass by.
Genies and devils and goblins!
Trespass not where Allah hath forbidden,
Else are ye traitors to Him whose Being exists of necessity.
I know the origin whence ye sprang,
From the soil of Mount Meru ye were born,
In the clouds, called the Beautiful Billowy Ones!
In the sky, the Pendent Ones!
In the fig-tree, the Peerers!
In water, the Crawlers!
In paths, the Up-Stickers!
I have Allah's mandate!
His Prophet is my prop;
The recording angels fight for me;
The four archangels are my brethren;
I live in a fort with seven walls of steel.
Descend angels and protect me
And cause my enemies to bow down;
Locked be the teeth and heart and spleen
Of all who purpose evil against me.
I know the origin of you spirits of evil:
Ye were sprung from the serpent Sakti-muna!
May ye be afflicted and distressed;
When ye gaze, may your eyes be blinded,
And may your going be shameful and grovelling.
Grandsire! (= Siva) thou who dwellest in bay and reaches,
*   upstream and down,*
Dwellest on mountain and in forest and on mound,
In ravine and valley and spring and tree and rock!
Take thy soldiery, thy people and thy children
To the shady tree at the land's end
At the foot of Mount Kaf.
Keep me from harm and destruction

Or thou shalt be smitten by the majesty of God's word.
For God and Muhammad and His saints and Prophets
And the angels forty-and-four and the four archangels
And the thirty chapters of the Kuran
Are with me.
Noah, guardian of earth!
Elias, guardian of wood!
Enoch, guardian of rock!
Lukman, guardian of iron!
Solomon, guardian of all living things!
I crave earth, water, wood and stone,
A place to build houses and hamlets and a country.
Ho! all living creatures,
We are all of one origin, all servants of God!
If ye harm or destroy me,
Ye shall be smitten by the word of God,
The miraculous power of Muhammad,
The sanctity of His saints and prophets,
By the four-and-forty angels,
And the four archangels
Grandsire, save me from harm!
If thy eye offend me, God shall blind thee;
If thy hand molest me, God shall break it;
If thy heart purpose evil towards me,
It shall be crushed by the Apostle of God.

Another incantation follows to open the doors of the seven heavens and the seven earths:

Genies infidel and Muslim!
You and I are of one origin, both servants of God.
But ye are born of hell-fire,
And I of the light of the Prophet;
Ye are children of Sakti-muna the serpent,
I am descended from the Prophet Adam;
Ye are followers of the Prophet Solomon,

THE RITUAL OF THE RICE-FIELD

I am a follower of the Prophet Muhammad.
You and I are servants of God.
Plague not the followers of Muhammad,
Else you will be traitors to God,
To His Prophet and the four archangels
And the angels forty-and-four.
Genies and devils and goblins!
Get hence to the big leafy tree at the land's end
At the foot of Mount Kaf,
Else ye will be traitors to Him who was from the beginning
To God's house at Jerusalem, the primal land.
My altar is strewn with clods red and black,
Genies! goblins! hence! and come ye not back.

For three or seven days after the ceremony no living thing may be killed nor even a branch broken.

Every year before starting to fell a clearing for rice, the Malay farmer takes a lump of benzoin on a plate wrapped in a white cloth as a present to the local magician, whose trust is 'first in God, next in His Prophet, and then in the magicians of old, the ancestral spirits who own the clumps and clods' of the locality.[1] This expert recites charms over the benzoin and returns it to the planter with traditional instructions. First he is to burn the benzoin in a bamboo cresset and fumigate his adzes and choppers, praying to the guardian spirits, male and female, newly dead and dead long since, to be cool and propitious. Then he is to stand erect facing eastward and look round at the four quarters of the heavens; he is to notice at which quarter his breath feels least faint and begin to fell in that direction. After one or two hacks at the trees he must cease work for the day.

One Perak account tells how the magician has a wood-

---

[1] Except where acknowledgment is made to other sources, the following account is based on two manuscripts writted by Perak headmen in 1912. It contains interesting details hitherto not noted in the Peninsula.

43

knife stuck into the earth and can tell from the incision
whether cultivation will prosper or not. He covers the hole
with a coconut-shell full of rice-paste and fences it with
sticks and brushwood. Next he cuts down a little under-
growth round the spot. A day or two later felling is begun.
If the ceremonies were omitted, the earth-spirit would send
fever, snake-bites, accidents from breaking branches or
from premature fire.

When the time comes to burn the clearing, the man gets
more benzoin from the magician, fumigates his torches,
lights them and cries thrice to spirits of all sorts, Indonesian,
Indian, Persian, Arabian, to goblins with a Sanskrit name,
to indigenous vampires, and goblins of the soil, saying that
the magician has duly informed them of his desire to burn,
that he himself has paid them due respect, and that trusting
to the luck of his instructor he hopes for a favourable breeze.
Very early in the morning after the burn he and his wife
and children must hurry to mitigate the smart of the half-
burnt clearing with water in which are steeped cold rice
from last night's meal, a slice from the cool heart of a
gourd, and other vegetable products chosen for their
natural frigidity or appropriately cool names. Also a little
maize should be planted. All this must be done before
Grannie Kemang can get up and sow rank weeds that will
flourish and provide hiding places for goblin pests. Before
quitting the clearing, one should pile and singe three rows
of the unburnt brushwood. Then one must go home and
wait three days before clearing the ground after the burn.

The next important occasion is the planting of the rice-
seed. In Perak and Kedah the time for this is taken from
observation of the Pleiades. 'When at 4.30 a.m. or there-
abouts a few grains of rice slip off the palm of the hand, the
arm being outstretched and pointed at the constellation, or
when, the arm being so directed, the bracelet slides down
the wrist, it is considered to be time to put down the rice

nursery.' In some places the planter is guided by observation of the sun, calculating from the time when it is thought to be exactly overhead at noon. Others 'keep the seed-grain in store for a certain definite period, that varies with the character of the grain and may be anything between four and seven months. . . . This period of rest is vital to the productive power of the seed.' The flooding of some stream, the fruiting of certain trees also afford rough local indications to supply the defect of the misleading Muhammadan lunar calendar.

A seed plot is chosen where the soil smells sweet. It is partitioned off by four sticks into a square of a prescribed size. Here both Sakai and Malays sometimes practise a method of divination. Water in a coconut shell and leaves are placed within the square. If the next morning finds the leaves undisturbed, the water unspilt and the frame unmoved, the spot is auspicious. It remains only to plant rice-seed in seven holes within the square as custom ordains, and this should be done during the dark of the moon, so that insects may not see to eat the seedlings.

A stick, if possible of a special kind of wood (termed the 'tortoise's chest') which has grown on an anthill, must be cut fresh on the morning of the ceremony to make the 'mother dibble'. It must be in length thrice the span between a woman's thumb and ring-finger and it must be peeled. A match or 'twin' for the mother dibble must also be prepared, of any wood, unpeeled, three cubits and three ring-fingers long. Another dibble is selected by the magician from the heap of dibbles brought by the planters. A pretty leafy shrub is got ready to make what the modern Malay calls a 'plaything' for the seed: probably, like the Maypole, it was once a symbol of fertility. The leader of the village mosque chants prayers for all souls. Then those present feast.

Next, with a white cloth about his head the magician squats, facing the east. The big toe of his right foot is above the big toe of his left, and he recites charms over benzoin. He fumigates the mother dibble, her 'match' and the other dibble, and sprinkles them with rice-paste, does the same to the other tools, and the same thrice to the earth in the middle of the chosen square. He holds out to the four quarters of heaven seven packets of sweet rice, seven sugar-canes, seven bamboos containing rice cooked in them, the Malay's most primitive cooking-pot, and rice parched, yellow and white. He lifts the mother dibble in both hands, holds it across his head, its point towards the right. After reciting spells he holds it above his shoulder point to earth, and digs it into the middle of the square, withdraws it and then plants it firm and erect in the hole. Next he plants the twin or duplicate, and then the leafy shrub. He ties the mother dibble, her 'twin' and the shrub together with bark, and decorates the mother dibble with a creeper whose name denotes increase. At the foot of the mother dibble he sets a bamboo containing rice from the freak ears most favoured for the rice-baby as certain to contain the rice soul, a rod of iron, a stone worn smooth in a waterfall, and three quids of betel. On the shrub he hangs seven packets of sweet rice, seven sugar canes, seven kinds of banana, seven sorts of jungle fruit, apparently to attract and keep the seven souls of the rice. He charms the third dibble and, before planting it also by the side of the mother dibble, uses it to make seven holes, saying as he makes them: 'Peace be unto thee, Solomon, Prophet of Allah, prince of all the earth! I would sow rice for seed. I pray thee protect it from all danger and mischance.'

After fumigating two handfuls of rice he holds it with his right hand above his left and sprinkles it with cool rice-water of the kind made for his burnt clearing and with the rice-paste used in all magical ceremonies. (In Negri Sembilan as he does this he recites a verse:

46

THE RITUAL OF THE RICE-FIELD

Rice-paste without speck!
I'll get gold by the peck!
I charm my rice crushed and in ear!
I'll get full grain within the year.)

The rice-paste is taken from a coconut shell (or in modern days from a soap-dish!), in which there have been steeped a nail and husked rice. It is applied with a brush of herbs whose vigorous growth or lucky names ('the reviver', 'the full one') are calculated to benefit the seed, body and soul. Going to the first hole the magician cries: 'Peace be unto thee, Solomon, Prophet of God, prince of all the earth! Peace be unto you, genies and goblins of the soil! Peace be unto my father the Sky and my mother the Earth! Peace be unto you, guardian father, guardian mother! I would send my child, daughter of Princess Splendid to her mother. I would bid her sail on the sea that is black, the sea that is green, the sea that is blue, the sea that is purple. For six months I send her, and in the seventh I will welcome her back. It is not seed I plant: it is rice-grain.' Holding his breath, he puts the seed into the seven holes. When he releases his breath, he does it gently and with averted face.

The rice-paste he buries beside the mother dibble and turns the coconut shell, its receptacle, upside down on the surface of the ground, fumigating it and passing a censer three times round it. Then he rises from his task.

Children rush to pick the sweet offerings from the shrub, though one offering at least must be left on its branches. The leader of the mosque intones prayers in honour of the Prophet. Men seize the dibbles, women the seed. With shouts and laughter the sexes strive to outdo one another in speed at their respective tasks. Before he goes home the owner of the field removes from the square the bamboo filled with rice for the evening meal of himself and his family; no stranger may partake of it.

If it is dry hill rice, the seed has been sown over the field from the first and no transplanting is required. If the rice is to be planted in an irrigated field, the seed is sown in a nursery and forty-four days later the young shoots are transplanted. That wet rice cultivation is less primitive is perhaps shown by the omission in many districts of all incantations at this function, though again seven bunches are planted first, along with a banana plant and three stems of the *Clinogyne grandis*, and a fence is built round them. (In Negri Sembilan the following invocation is addressed to spirits:

> *O Langkesa! O Langkesi!*
> *Spirits of the field ye are four!*
> *Counting me we are five!*
> *Hurt not nor harm my child!*
> *Break faith and ye shall be stricken*
> *By the iron that is strong,*
> *By the majesty of Pagar Ruyong*
> *(Home of our royal house),*
> *By the thirty chapters of the Quran.*
> *Allah fulfil my curse!*)

After this preliminary rite no work is done for the rest of the day. On the morrow the seedlings are planted out by women, who must neither drop the young plants nor speak. A wooden dibble is used in remote districts; elsewhere a dibble with a steel point that bears the euphemistic name of 'the goat's hoof'. 'This instrument carries from five to nine seedlings at once and is used seven times in quick succession.' While each of seven bunches of seedlings is being planted the tongue must be pressed against the roof of the mouth: before cutting the seven ears that contain the rice souls, the magician will press the thumb of the right hand against the roof of the palate. At this season a propitiatory sacrifice is sometimes offered to the earth spirits. If dry rice is being cultivated, this is done about the time the grain begins to swell. From about the fourth month of its growth no stranger may enter the field. At this stage the stalk has five joints only and it must be fumigated daily till the grain appears. Spells and amulets are used to protect the crop from pests. An albino rat placed in a cage on the field will keep away rats.

As soon as the ear has swollen large, the farmer cooks sweet rice in a bamboo and invites the magician, the leader of the mosque, and other worthies to the feast of 'splitting the bamboo'. Nightly now rubbish and stinking herbs are burnt to scare evil spirits.

When the crop is ripe for harvest, the magician has to 'take the souls of the rice'. For two evenings he walks round the edge of the field, coaxing and *collecting them*. On the third he enters the field to search for their host, looking about for ears of royal yellow, certain types of freak ear reminding one of a veiled or laughing princess, ears on stalks interlaced or seven-jointed, ears from stalks with a lucky bird's nest at the root. When he has found a suitable host, he ties seven stalks with bark and fibre and many-coloured thread having a nail attached to it, and slips the nail into the middle of the bunch. He may plant a leafy stem of sugar-cane in the middle of the chosen sheaf as a prop for the stalks. Thrice before the cutting of the seven stalks is performed the magician walks round them bidding malicious earth spirits avaunt:

'Goblins of latter days! Goblins of the beginning! Goblins one hundred and ninety! Goblins under my feet and subjection! Goblins that creep into baskets and round stalks! Goblins of hill and mountain and plain! Goblins mine! Get ye back and aside or I will curse you.'

Early the next morning the leader of the mosque mounts a covered shelter in the field and intones prayers in honour of the Prophet. A feast follows. When evening is about to fall, the magician and an assistant and the farmer walk up to the plant chosen the day before. A puzzle ring is carried to hang on the stalks. The magician, his head covered with a white cloth, draws near. Taking care lest his shadow fall on the seven stalks, he fumigates them and, sprinkling rice-paste, grasps them gingerly, hiding in his palm a tiny blade, whose handle is carved in the shape of a bird for disguise. He bows his head to the ground and mutters a traditional invocation:

> *Soul of my child, Princess Splendid!*
> *I sent you to your mother for six months, to receive you grow-ing tall in the seventh month.*
> *The time is fulfilled, and I receive you.*
> *I told you to sail to the sea that is black, the sea that is green, the sea that is blue, and the sea that is purple,*
> *To the land of Rome, to India, China, and Siam.*
> *Now I would welcome you up into a palace hall,*
> *To a broidered mat and carpet.*
> *I would summon nurses and followers,*
> *Subjects and soldiers and court dignitaries for your service;*
> *I would assemble horses and elephants, ducks and geese, buffaloes and goats and sheep with all their din.*
> *Come, for all is ready!*
> *I would call you hither,*
> *Soul of my child, Princess Splendid!*
> *Come! my crown and my garland! flower of my delight!*
> *I welcome you up to a palace-hall,*
> *To a broidered mat and carpet.*
> *Soul of my child, Princess Splendid!*
> *Come! I would welcome you!*
> *Forget your mother and wet-nurse.*
> *White and black and green and blue and purple! get ye aside!*
> *Brightness of genie and devil begone!*
> *The real brightness is the brightness of my child.*

THE RITUAL OF THE RICE-FIELD

Clearly the four seas must symbolize the black earth of the newly tilled fields, and the carpet of green rice-plants changing tint from light to dark until the harvest.

The magician lifts his head. Skyward and all around he gazes for the advent of the rice-soul. With the sound of a breeze it appears either in the form of a grasshopper or other insect or in the shape of a girl, Grannie Kemang. If it fails at first to come, the repetition of the most coaxing lines of the invocation three times is certain to fetch it. The magician holds his breath, shuts his eyes, sets his teeth, and with one cut severs the ears from the seven stalks. Like a midwife holding a new-born child, he puts the ears in his lap and swaddles them in a white cloth. This rice baby he hands to the owner of the land to hold. He cuts seven more clusters of grain from round the plant whence 'she' was taken and puts them along with an egg and a golden banana into the basket prepared for the baby. The rice-baby is cradled among brinjal leaves, a stone and a piece of iron, and under a canopy of cool creepers and bark and fibre and coloured thread. The magician smears the seven stalks from which the ears were cut with clay, 'as medicine for their hurt from the knife', and hides them under neighbour stalks that are whole. Then facing the east, he touches the maimed stalks and cries:

> Ho ancestresses whose rice-fields shone at the coming of our first
>   king!
> Grow here, maidens, in clumps!
> Establish your home here!
> If the seven tiers of heaven are shaken,
> Then only shall my child, Princess Splendid, be shaken;
> If the seven layers of earth are shaken,
> Then only shall my child, Princess Splendid, be shaken;
> Else shall she be established as rock, firm as iron
> From this world unto the world hereafter,

THE MALAY MAGICIAN

Established in limbs and body with father and mother.
Only if the Prophet be parted from Allah
Shall you be parted from me.

The magician kisses the rice-stalks and heads the procession carrying the rice-baby home. The farmer is addressed as the father of the baby and his wife as the mother. She and her children are waiting and, as she takes the basket from her husband, the woman exclaims: 'Dear heart! My life! My child! How I have longed for your return from your voyage! Every day of your absence, every month, all the year I've missed you. Now you've returned safe and sound! Come! Your room is ready.' She kisses the rice-baby three times. The magician fumigates and sprinkles a spot for the cradle. Then he takes the egg out of the cradle and breaks it. If there is an empty space at the top of the egg, it is a poor omen; if at either side of it, a good; but if the shell is quite full, the omen is so good that it must be greeted with an offering of yellow rice and a spatch-cock. The egg and the golden banana must be eaten by the farmer and his family, and no one else may taste them. For three days the household must keep vigil, the fire may not be quenched, the food in the cooking-pots may not be finished, no one may go down from the house or ascend to it. Thus all the precautions fitting for a new-born child must be observed. During the three days following these birth tabus, one small basket of ears a day may be reaped, and the reaper must work silently, not gaze around, and guard against his shadow falling on the plants as he would guard against another's shadow falling on his own. On the seventh day reaping may begin in earnest, but the yield for that day is devoted to a feast in honour of the spirits of dead magicians, the forebears who have charge of the district.

The rice won on the seventh day is trodden out on a mat, and winnowed in a sieve. Then the grain is placed on a mat in the middle of the garden along with brinjal leaves, a stone from a waterfall, an iron nail, a candle-nut, three cockle-shells, a creeper and the inverted rattan stand of a cooking-pot on which is put a coconut shell full of water (to quench the thirst of the parching grain). Around this stand the grain is spread, nor may it be left unwatched until the sun has dried it.

In some parts of the Peninsula there is a 'harvest dance that forms part of the procedure of gathering in the rice. The performers are a band of some fifteen or twenty young children, both boys and girls, who carry winnowing-sieves and other tools of the harvester. The troop is invited forward by an old woman taking up her position on the threshing-screen and singing to the children, who respond by dancing and putting questions for the old lady to answer in verse. When the spectators are weary of the dancing and singing, the performance is brought to an end in the following very curious way. The girl-leader of the children's chorus sings a verse that purports to be a charm "making all things brittle". Having done so (doubtless with the idea of making the threshing easier) she leads her band of dancers to the screen by way of testing the efficacy of the magic. The children tramp and stamp on the screen; and when a lath has shown its brittleness by breaking, the charm is supposed to have done its work and the dance ends.'

The next process is to pound the rice in a wooden mortar. Again the mortar must be hung with bark, black fibre, coloured thread and cool-named leaves. Allah and the Prophet are invoked. The pestle crushes the grain slowly three, five or seven times, and then may work at ordinary speed. The rice crushed, the 'eldest child of the year', is cooked in a spray-hung pot and eaten at a feast.

The last and biggest feast of the rice year is 'the Malay harvest home. Each planter keeps open house in turn, when all his friends come to help him tread out his grain. Even reverend elders assume for the time the manner of children and verses are bandied with the gentle licence characteristic of Malay junketings.' Games, theatricals (and formerly buffalo fights) formed part of the celebrations. Tithes are paid to the mosque and fees to the magician.

The magician presides over the first storing of the grain in the barn. Again, brinjal leaves, a stone from a waterfall, a piece of iron, a candle-nut or better three candle-nuts, a plant with a fine healthy name, three cockle-shells, a piece of torch, all covered with the ancestral rice-measure and the measure covered with the rattan stand of a cooking-pot hung with bark and fibre and coloured thread—on these solid soul-strengthening foundations he pours the grain from the three basketfuls of rice cut near the sheaf whence the rice-baby was taken. The shepherd of souls has performed his final task and the remainder of the grain is left for the farmer to pile.

Some of the ears that go to make up the rice-baby will be mixed with next year's seed and some with next year's magic rice-paste used at all functions by the Malay magician.

This account of the ritual of the rice-year in the Malay Peninsula can be supplemented from other sources. About 1830 in Province Wellesley the rice-seed was measured twice before being sown in the nursery 'in order to ascertain that none had escaped preternaturally'. There, too, sometimes seven stalks were cut for the rice-baby, sometimes two only, a male and a female, on each side of which a gold or silver ring was tied before they were wrapped together in a white cloth. The most notable point in the Perak account is that the farmer and his wife are regarded as the father and mother of the rice-soul. In Malacca the sheaf from which the baby is cut is called the mother, treated like a woman after childbirth and reaped by the farmer's wife. In ancient Greece there was confusion as to the moment when Demeter, the corn-mother, changed into Persephone, the corn-daughter, and in many other countries the bucolic mind has glozed over this difficulty.

The charming of hatchets, the dibble cut from a special tree likely by sympathetic magic to influence the quality of the rice-plant, the dibbling of seven holes in a special plot, the holidays prescribed after felling and sowing and reaping, the seven ears for the rice-soul, the various communal feasts throughout the rice-year, all these are found among the proto-Malay tribes of Malaya.

In Negri Sembilan, where matrilineal custom laughs at the prosciptions of Islam, girls and men bandy Malay *pantun*, half-verse, half-riddle, one with another as they work in the fields. Comparison with planting rites in other lands has suggested that riddles are a survival of a tabu language, employed not to frighten the soul of a cereal by direct reference to the processes of agriculture.

The symbolism of the ritual will be clear to any one who has grasped the primitive Malay notion of the soul. The soul of the rice in the field is of the same stuff as the soul of a villager and, figured in anthropomorphic form, is treated with the care lavished on a new-born child.

VII

THE SHAMAN'S SEANCE

THE main details of a Malay *séance* resemble those of the Mongolian: the beating of tambourines, frantic incantations, the rustle and voices of invisible beings, the expulsion or sucking out of spirits of disease or the revelation of future events, the medium oblivious of what has passed during his trance, the sacrificial offerings for unseen powers. Originally in the Far East a trance induced by the thud of drums lifted the shaman to heaven, there to discover a client's future or to receive plant or flower to cure a patient's illness—an adventure that is one of the commonest exploits of the hero in Indian popular tales. Later from India came the idea of gods and spirits descending from heaven to possess the shaman, when for his switch of grass or leaves there might be substituted in Kelantan figures from the Indo-Javanese shadow-play.

The trance has been the essential feature of the shaman's *séance*, though like other folk he may have spirit animals or other familiars at his call. The prime helper for a Malay shaman was a dead predecessor in tiger form (p. 12). In Negri Sembilan it is recognized that this helper needed no summons, though at a Perak court ceremony he was invoked to descend (p. 70). Perhaps the ignorance of observers has led accounts to overlook that the shaman becomes the tiger-spirit, putting off his humanity to enter the unseen world and receive the revelations of gods or spirits. From Perak and Selangor it is recorded that a magician at a *séance* will growl and sniff and crawl under mats and lick the naked body of a patient, his growls and movements showing that he has been transformed and so far from being possessed by his spirit helper has obtained control of it. During a Kelantan *séance*, it is alleged, a tiger appears at least once, though experts debate whether it is the real animal or only a were-tiger. A Kelantan shaman will even refuse to hold a *séance* in a town because the tiger it must attract might be shot, a reluctance calculated to corroborate the belief that the shaman, if a male, has or should have had the power of transforming himself into one. To add verisimilitude to this primitive folk-lore (which occurs also in Vedic India), no dog or cat is allowed at a *séance* for fear the shaman seize and devour it. Nor may the tiger-spirit be offended by such an emblem of mortality as a piece of leather! The long lineage of the Malay tiger-spirit can be inferred from comparison with the boar which every Samoyed shaman is thought to have as his familiar and lead about by a magic belt.

In Malaya, however, this animal familiar has been associated for centuries with other spirits or replaced by them. Some Pahang wizards have for their helpers elves and echo-spirits; Kelantan wizards may have the Hoverers (*mambang*) in the Yellow Sunset or a child Guardian of Estuaries with a Javanese title (*Kuda*) derived from Hindu Majapahit in the fourteenth century. In Kelantan, too, a female shaman will have to assist her in sorcery the Ghost of the Lad with the Cut Throat, aboriginal spirits of the argus-pheasant and pig-tailed monkey, and mightiest of all, Kala, the Hindu god of death, whom Islam has degraded to be Grandad Black Genie. The shaman invokes indiscriminately benevolent and malignant powers to his aid.

At the Perak court the tiger familiar continued to play a

part down to recent times in the ceremony for reviving spirits immanent in the royal drums and trumpets. His survival is ingeniously explained. He was invoked in complimentary phrases inspired by the knowledge that 'Ali, son-in-law of the Prophet, is the Lion of God and by the assumption that the Malayan lion is the tiger! Oblivious now of his role as a ghostly shaman, Perak peasants rank him today with the Boy with the Long Lock of Hair, the Blackamoor Boy, the Young Hornbill, the Hoverer in the Sunset and 'Omar Ummaya, the mythical hero of an Arabic romance! A common set created out of village annals and village learning.

The great guardian spirits of Perak (or by Muslim euphemism the genies of the royal trumpets) are also a motley crowd. These familiars of the Sultan and the State Shaman include Brahma, and Visnu and Indra, the prophet Solomon and the caliph 'Ali. Yet some of them, too, are creatures of local legend, the Princeling of the Rolling Sea and Four Children of the Prince of the Iron Pestle. Most of them are powers of the air with Sanskrit and Persian titles taken from Malay translations of popular romances from the Deccan. One, Mardan Ardekas, is a mythical steed from the tale of *Shams al-Bahrain*!

Among these exalted spirits the State Shaman and his royal assistants moved with the ease of accomplished courtiers, honouring each of them with head-dress of appropriate colour, green for the Sultan of the World of Flowers, yellow for Visnu and white for Brahma. As the Sultan Muda or State Shaman fell into a trance, twelve musicians at once would beat their drums and cry in the language of literary romance to the spirit to be invoked:

> *Ho, Lord of the world!*
> *Sultan, prince of miraculous power!*
> *Prince, divinity of clear vision!*

THE SHAMAN'S SEANCE

Prince of pools of heavenly brightness!
Lord of the world of dark plains!
Hearken, prince, to the words of thy slaves!
Hearken, prince, to their wind-borne cry!
Arise and come to our jewelled curtains,
Come and enter the (shaman's) ear posy.

Spirit after spirit may descend at a *séance* before the advent of the one it is desired to consult. And the shaman may regard himself as actually becoming the spirit invoked, and if it is female, amuse his audience by impersonating a woman's gait. From this and from the antics of magicians incorporating their tiger familiar, it might appear that every spirit enters the body of the medium. On the contrary Malays explain that a spirit alights on the back, neck or shoulder of the magician, on his grass aspergillum or on the flame of a candle. Access more intimate would cause sickness or death.

The ritual of a Malay *séance* will be as elaborate as the knowledge of the shaman can devise and the means of his patron afford. A *séance* should occupy an uneven number of days, not less than three or more than nine, and the spectators present should also make up an uneven number, which must not vary from night to night. If the performance is conducted in a shed, the building, at any rate in Kelantan, is orientated east and west, unlike the homes of earthly folk, which to avoid the sunset region of death face north and south. The first post must be felled and erected by the patron of the *séance*; the rest of the building along with its decoration may be done by relatives and friends but not by hired labour. So, too, food for the shaman and the spirits should be prepared by the family.

The shaman will fumigate the tapers to be use l, then whistle towards the west and hold two lighted tapers crossed, while reciting a short invocation. Next, chanting,

59

he and his assistants enter the shed and pace three times round the enclosure corded off for them, while parched rice is scattered in all directions, making an uncanny rustle that attracts spirits. Removing his own share from the food prepared the shaman recites words appropriate for an offering. He blows towards the four points of the compass and continues his recitation with hands joined before his face and palms upturned. He then chooses from the plates rice saffron and parched, an egg and betel, sets them on a banana leaf, sprinkles them and puts them on the ground before the main house-pillar as a gift for spirits of the soil. Here he may chant how offerings are made to Father Sky and Mother Earth, to all the Saints of Islam and to Siva, chief of Islam's infidel genies, whom he entreats to recall his followers that are plaguing the sick man. His assistant now starts the music. Every Tantra ought to begin with the story of the creation and go on to deal with the worship of the gods. So, after reciting the (now Muslim) order of creation and the magician's place in time, the assistant shaman bows before Father Sky and Mother Earth, pays tribute to the saints and miracle-workers of Islam and to the Shaikhs who guard the four quarters of the world and entreats Kala, the Hindu god of death, now addressed as the spectre Huntsman and now as the Black Chief of Muslim Genies, to spare the patient. The Young Bachelor of the Orchard and the seven Black Princesses with wings of bale are bidden not to sit chuckling at him. To genies that bring fever, genies that cause knife-like agony, genies that scrape all into death's net, genies that prepare the shroud and the yawning grave, to all the powers of darkness on land and sea he chants his adjuration. Sometimes in imitation of the credentials of Muslim teachers, the shaman and his assistant will now recite the names of former magicians, their teachers and ancestors.

After that, brush in hand, the pair dance in turn or together to the thud of music, that dies down when the dancers chant. Or the assistant may cry upon beneficent spirits to descend, while his chief with closed eyes whirls his (or her) head frantically until dizzy and possessed. If the *séance* is to continue on other nights, neither music nor dance nor head-whirling may cause the performer to fall or pretend to fall completely into a trance. It is sufficient merely to get into touch with the spirit world.

On the second night fresh offerings will be made with richer dainties, glutinous rice, coconuts, roast chicken. Once more homage is paid to ancestors. The shamans dance again. Incense is burnt and tapers are lit. The assistant calls upon spirits to possess his chief, who leaping about convulsively on his mat utters an unintelligible spirit language. He embodies his tiger familiar which may become visible to the credulous. Every time the shaman recovers from possession, his assistant demands who the spirit was and whence he came. The artifice of the performance becomes patent to the sceptic when the dancers rise and indulge in burlesque in order to relieve tension in the audience.

On a third night there will be more dancing and more invocations. After his first trance the shaman will examine the patient, brushing him with his bunch of grass and sprinkling him with water. To make assurance doubly sure he supplements the diagnosis supplied by spirits by gazing at the flame of a taper or at water in jars, in case he may divine the cause and cure for the malady. Again he may dance and fall into a trance. Recovering he will brush and sprinkle the sick man, suck at his body or rub it with medicinal leaves and a bezoar stone. He may tell the patient to drink charmed water from an inverted jar for seven days. Every Tantric ritual should close with the four modes of union with the Supreme Spirit. So now the Muslim successor of the Hindu will start another chant full of pantheistic Sufi lore, declaring that man's body is the house of Allah

61

and no place for spirits of evil (p. 85). Finally he will coax the spirit that is plaguing the sufferer into his own body (whence his familiar can expel it) or aboard a model ship or even a model mosque, that is loaded with every part of a fowl, including feathers and entrails, and set it adrift on a river. Before the *séance* ends, a bowl of holy water is passed round, and next morning all the participators are drenched with consecrated water employed during the ritual, the idea apparently being the cleansing from dangerous influences, which in the Vedic religion led the celebrant of the Soma sacrifice and his wife to cross a river. Another precaution is to loosen knots tied in threads and fronds in order to release all present from the assault of invisible foes.[1]

If the health of the patient improves another *séance* may be held after the lapse of a week or two. If he recovers, a thank-offering is made, actuated no doubt by fear of punishment for omission but containing also the germ of a free-will sacrifice of gratitude.

The use of the shaman's trance has been most common in areas like Siberia, where arctic hysteria is prevalent, and among the Malays, many of whom are *latah*. Both of these nervous maladies will lead sufferers to mimic the words and gestures of those who startle them, to strip themselves naked and utter the obscenities of the subconscious mind. Contact with the spirit-world, made manifest by such nervous seizures, has qualified man and woman in many primitive tribes to become medium, exorcist and diviner. 'He stripped off his clothes and prophesied before Samuel and lay down naked all that day and all that night, wherefore they say, "Is Saul also among the prophets?" '

[1] A converse example of this magic is a method of capturing and controlling the maleficent aura (*bahdi*) of a slain deer. Sweep first a gun, then a branch, then the noose in which the animal was caught over its carcass from muzzle to hind legs. Then quickly slip the noose round a stake and fasten it there.

THE SHAMAN'S SÉANCE

All the characteristics of the Malay shaman appear in patients suffering from protracted hysterical delirium. For both, visual hallucinations are especially visions of animals and fantastic processions of ghosts and demons. The patient will utter meaningless words borrowed subconsciously from several languages. One woman had to have a splinter cut out of her finger and 'suddenly saw herself beside a brook in a beautiful meadow plucking flowers'. Another 'gradually lost her abnormal sensitiveness and six months later was caught cheating at a *séance*, concealing small objects in her dress and throwing them up in the air, wanting to restore belief in her supernatural powers'. A diagnosis of these cases of hysterical delirium by Jung might have been made from study of the Malay shaman alone.

There is, however, an impassable gulf between the hysterical visions of an adolescent mind and the calculated ritual of the trained shaman of maturer years, when intellect has taken the place of lost inspiration. One Perak shaman, possessed by a spirit, yet remembers court etiquette sufficiently to bow to members of the royal family. Another, toothless, asks why the betel-nut has not been pounded for him as the genie possessing him is stricken in years!

In Kelantan the *séance* at which the state is cleansed is conducted by five or six shamans, male and female, one of them playing the part of a "princess", namely of Siva's Sakti, personification of the principle of life, without which Siva and crops would be dead. This *séance* must be a survival of orgiastic Tantrism when the part of the "princess" was played by a nude woman and no other medium was required for union with God. The chief assistant of the "princess" is still called the bridegroom. (P. 154.)

VIII

SACRIFICE

T HE idea of sacrificial offerings obsesses the mind of the Malay peasant, believing as he does every object to be the repository of a spirit and every phenomenon to be the manifestation of a spirit. In Pahang villagers will sacrifice an animal so that its blood dropping on the ground may cause a downpour of rain to cease, or, if an animal cannot be procured, they will cut their own hands or feet. An egg and a plantain will placate a crocodile. Rice, plantains and cigarettes cast on a rock will conciliate the spirit of a rapid. The actor throws a quid of betel on to the roof of his playhouse for the white genies of the air and buries another for the black genies of the soil. The miner along with other food will present black rice and portions of a black fowl, cooked and uncooked, to the spirits of a tin mine—where ore is black like gunpowder. Rice planters erect an altar in their fields and propitiate the spirits of the dark soil with the flesh of a black goat. The cock offered to Siva should be yellow. The goat sacrificed for a sacred animal or a Muslim saint or a revered ancestor should be white. The proto-Malay Mantra will carry two white fowls to a hill-top reputed to be the haunt of a kindly spirit. One he will release, the other he will kill and put on a tray of food to be laid on the ground or hung from a tree. Then he will silently intimate his heart's desire and eat some of the food on the spot to bring himself into communion with the spirit.

The humblest offering is selected in accordance with traditional rules. For some the kinds of rice should be

64

seven, a mystic number hallowed in ancient Babylon. Five was another sacred number and some Malay offerings contain five quids of betel, five cigarettes and five tapers to light the spirits to their fare.

Even the position of an offering is significant, its exposure on a beach, its burial in the soil or suspension from a tree. A Selangor fisherman will hang three receptacles for meat, vegetables, betel and cigarettes, one on the shore, one on a shoal half-way to the fishing-ground and one on his trap, aiming thus to placate the spirits of earth, beach and sea. It is round the main pillar of a house about to be built that the Malay deposits the head and feet of goat or buffalo, a practice recalling the theory that bisected pieces of man or animal guard any space between them from the incursion of evil powers. 'When Peleus captured the city of Iolcus, he is said to have taken the king's wife, cut her in two and then led his army between the pieces into the city.' On building a new house Dayaks used formerly to sacrifice a slave-girl. The sacrifice of slaves, often with horrible circumstance, was common in Indonesia on the erection of a house, at a chief's funeral and on return from war. Underlying these sacrifices are several discrepant ideas. Oldest of all may be that of a union between man and the spirit or god he would invoke. It is said that when the Telugus deck a buffalo for sacrifice, it is not as a gift to a carnivorous god but as the god's representative, whose blood will secure his presence at the place of sacrifice. Chinese, too, would swear an oath loudly into the severed ear of a victim in which amorphous deity was made incarnate. Such evidence is lacking in Malaya. But in ceremonies held to coax away maleficent beings, the risk of a bond between them and the celebrant, if all partook of the sacrifice, appears to be consciously avoided. On a tray of food for spirits plaguing a sick man there was observed a faked quid with betel-nut replaced by nutmeg, gambir by mace and lime by oil, though the quid to be chewed by the physician and ejected on the patient's back was genuine. And a similar idea of avoiding any bond between evil spirits and their supplicants may account for the cooking of food for a state sacrifice in Kelantan not at home but where three roads meet.

Another ancient idea (found also in Vedic religion) is that supernatural beings having human wants suffer privation and become feeble, unless they are given the same food as mortals.[1] So periodical sacrifices are made by district or state or on a mine-field not to placate maleficent powers but to provide sustenance for the guardian spirits of the territory, and the shaman being the accredited medium for communication with Father Sky and Mother Earth and with the spirits of ancestors, the gods of the Hindu pantheon and the genies of Islam he is employed to hold a *séance* to invite them to a feast.

The desire to promote friendly relations between the villagers and the spirits of a district is clear from an account of a feast held in Upper Perak 'when the grain in the rice-fields was beginning to swell'. It is a ceremony particularly interesting, because in it have survived the elements of one of mankind's oldest rituals: a victim without spot, a feast in which all partake before the altar, the blood that may not fall upon the ground, the offering that must be utterly consumed and that no stranger may approach, the celebration by night or before dawn. It is a feast of the settled agriculturist claiming a right to his fields and owing a duty to the gnomes and goblins that haunt them.

For this district feast every one contributed a measure of rice and two coconuts. Candles were lit and the shaman burnt incense. Next he invoked 'the ancestral spirits, genies and goblins, owners of the earth and water of the district', and prayed them to cherish all from danger and hurt. He

[1] If mishap at sea reveals that the soul of his boat is weak, the Patani fisherman engaged a magician to feed it with offerings laid on each rib.

informed them that he was slaughtering a pink buffalo
(sacred to the Malay as to the Mongol), an animal without
blemish and with horns the size of a man's closed fist—and
an animal which from its colour was almost certainly intended primarily for Father Sky. Nose, eyes, ears, mouth,
hooves, legs and shoulders, tongue, tail, heart and liver
were set aside. From the flesh of the carcass seven kinds of
food were prepared: soused, boiled, fried, roast and so on,
with one portion left raw—the raw perhaps as in China for
earth spirits and the cooked for ancestral spirits. On the top
of a seven-tiered altar were placed the blood, the parts set
aside, the seven kinds of meat, seven cooked and seven raw
eggs with seven vessels of water. On the five central tiers
were spread sweetmeats; on the lowest tier twenty-five
cigarettes and twenty-five quids of betel. The food not
offered on the altar was eaten by those present; none might
be removed. At dusk the Muslim villagers went home,
leaving the shaman and his assistants. After circumambulat-
ing the altar, he burnt incense again and waving a white
cloth invited spirits to the feast. Seven times he hailed them
and then departed. For seven days no stranger might enter
the parish, no one might throw anything into it or take anything out, no one might use unseemly language or cause
leaf or branch to wither.

As in India and in China, so in Malaya the spirits of districts came to be subservient to the spirit of the State; in
China this supernatural centralization is said to have been
effected in the second century before Christ. In Malaya
these spirits of a state commanded sacrifices either at the
uncertain times of epidemics or else every third, fifth or
seventh year. The ceremonies (*palis* corrupted *pĕlas* in
Perak) used to be triennial in Perak and Kelantan. 'The
main line of development in ritual' has been described as
being 'from the propitiation or insulation of evil influences
to the conciliation of beneficent powers'. In the Perak

ceremony, however, there was a divided aim, the sacrifice designed to decoy evil spirits to the open sea being also offered to beneficent powers. So, too, in the Kelantan ceremony not only ancestral spirits but spirits of the soil whose caprice can ruin crops both had their altars.

In Perak, state and parish magicians would assemble at a village below the rapids of the river that gives the country its name. For seven days they conducted *séances* to summon friendly spirits. Then the head and other portions of a pink buffalo were piled on a raft, which set off downstream. Appropriate magicians manned the four leading rafts, which were prepared for the four great classes of spirits. The foremost raft carried a branching tree (*pokok pĕrah*)— of the species used for tree-burial (p. 21); erected and supported by stays it was for the shamans' familiars. The fifth raft bore Muslim elders. The sixth carried the sacred drums and trumpets of the royal band. Lastly came the assistant of the State Shaman with his followers. As they floated down-river, the magicians waved white cloths and invoked the spirits of the district passed to come aboard and consume the offerings. Whenever a mosque was reached, they halted for one night; a *séance* was held and the villagers slaughtered a buffalo, placing its head on one of the four leading rafts and eating the rest. At the estuary the rafts were abandoned and allowed to drift to the Straits of Malacca. Both the state and parish magicians alighted at their home villages, leaving it to assistants to escort to the sea the rafts with their visible freight of grisly heads and unseen freight of greedy spirits.

In the Kelantan ceremony there were the customary *séances*. Offerings identical with those in the Perak ritual were set not on rafts but on a seven-tiered pyramid of bamboo, along with flour models of a ship, a hoe or plough, a rice-mortar, a pestle, a basket and seven pairs of animals. For earth-spirits there was a small square altar table (*tabak*) where were placed the same offerings minus the blood and offal and the models of animals. Ancestral spirits were offered four jars of water with food and gold and silver powder. Sweetmeats were hung up for spirits of the air. There was a model ship with food for spirits of the sea. And there were five cressets of splayed bamboo with vegetable offerings for village spirits. The flat platform altar and the splayed cressets remind one of the widespread evolution of the altar proper and the idol developed from a post or monolith beside the altar. In Polynesia, also, 'beside the larger temple altars there were smaller altars, some resembling a round table, supported by a single post in the ground: occasionally the carcass of the hog presented in sacrifice was placed on the large altar, while the heart and some other internal parts were laid on the smaller.'

The sacrifice that most clearly illustrates the idea of providing sustenance for spirits liable to hunger is a sacrifice for regalia and musical instruments. In China two thousand years ago blood was poured upon war-gongs and in Celebes the Bugis would sacrifice to regalia and smear them with blood. The same superstition has led the shaman at a Kelantan *séance* to touch the viol (*rĕbab*) of his orchestra with rice and betel and pour water in and around its gongs. In Perak feeding the spirits immanent in the regalia was a most elaborate court ceremony, when shrouded musicians thronged the palace, invoking his or her familiar. The State Shaman, the Sultan Muda, sat veiled with a bunch of grass in his hand, while the chief musician (*biduan; mödwŏn Cham*) called upon the guardian genies of Perak in order of precedence to descend and bring their thousand attendant spirits.

'Come!' he chanted. 'Come down to the gate of this world! Pass in procession to the posy, your place to alight. In your might lies the might of our Sultan. Come! Descend on the posy of the Sultan Muda and enter your jewelled curtain.' As each spirit entered the posy, the chant was hushed and the sound of the tambourines was quenched.

Meanwhile some humbler shaman would be invoking his tiger familiar: 'Warrior! Son of a Warrior! Matchless in power! Come, my lord! Come, my life! Descend on this posy, your alighting place, and enter your jewelled curtain. Come! by the blessing of 'Ali, the spirit who hangs at the door of the sky.'

When the tiger-spirit came, the village magician who had invoked him would turn about seven times and leap and growl, as his familiar demanded why he had been summoned, and he would make answer, 'You have been invited because our lord has got ready a hall and is inviting the Sultan of the Impalpable Air and all his followers to a feast upon the morrow and hopes that no harm will befall them on the way.'

Speaking through the shaman, the familiar replied, 'It is well. I and my subjects can attend. The bad I will not bring.'

So spirit after spirit was raised and invited, until the Sultan Muda gave the signal to retire.

The next morning the Sultan Muda, his assistant and their drummers went with rice-paste, turmeric and censers to direct the building of a nine-tiered pyramid, surmounted by an image of Jatayu (offspring of Visnu's Garuda) that lives on dew. It was adorned with streamers and hung with palm-leaf boxes of rice, cakes, sugar-cane and bananas. On the topmost tier was put the severed head of a pink buffalo, surrounded by water-vessels. Another altar on sixteen posts was erected, with offerings for spirits not connected with the destinies of the State. Two bamboo cressets served to hold food for the spirits of Muslim miracle-workers (kramat).

At dusk the Sultan Muda mounted and waved from the pyramid. Other magicians waved beside the altar and cressets. Then the assistant State Shaman, the Raja Kechil Muda, fell into a trance and with shouts ascended to the mat spread for him. Twelve musicians beat their drums and chanted invocations to the genies to leave the pools and plains of the spirit world and enter the posies and jewelled curtains prepared for them. After a rest for refreshment the magicians renewed their invocations. The music of their orchestras was answered by the thud of all the royal drums and the blare of the royal trumpets. On the right of the presiding magicians sat virgin princesses holding sacrificial offerings on their laps, on the left young unmarried princes supporting the regalia. And now the two chief magicians did obeisance to the regalia, offered delicacies to the 'thousand genies' and poured upon the royal drums and into the royal trumpets drink that vanished miraculously as though imbibed. Finally towards dawn the Sultan Muda and his attendant magicians fetched the ruler of the state and bathing His Highness bathed in his sacred person the genies that presided over the fate of his kingdom. Respect for the numbers seven and nine goes back to Mesopotamia, but the nine tiers of the pyramid used for the ruler's lustration here and on his installation may be a forgotten symbol of the stages up which the pre-Hindu shaman climbed to heaven in his ecstatic trance. Many of Perak guardian genies inhabit the sky.

Notes. (1) The account of the Perak ritual of feeding spirits immanent in the regalia was written for me by Raja Haji Yahya of Chendriang. In *Life and Customs*, Part I (Papers on Malay Subjects) Kuala Lumpor, Mr. R. J. Wilkinson without evidence transferred it into a ritual for curing sickness.

(2) Negritos say only the tiger-spirit enters the shaman's body; other spirits sit on his knee or shoulder (*Negritos of Malaya*, I. H. N. Evans, Cambridge, 1937).

(3) The cosmic tree appears in the Dongsonian spirit-boat, the Perak raft p. 68 *supra*) and the boat of the diver for fish (Frontispiece *supra*).

IX

MAGICIAN AND SUFI

'Siva the Teacher, the Light of Muhammad
and Lukman al-Hakim were the magicians
of old. I am the fourth magician.'

Malay Charm Book

How tolerant Islam was of magic is shown by a passage in the *Ninety-Nine Laws* of Perak compiled in the eighteenth century by a family of Sayids or descendants of the Prophet, which numbered among its members several Muslim saints. 'Muslims,' it is laid down, 'must feed the district judge, the officials of the mosque, the magician and the midwife. The *muezzin* is king in the mosque and the magician is king in the house of the sick, in the rice-field and on the mine. . . . A parish magician must be long-headed, suave, industrious and truthful, and he must not have intrigues with women. If a person is sick, he must attend immediately. His reward is that he escapes taxation and forced labour'—like the priests in Vedic India. And the Laws go on to prescribe the magician's fees for taking care of village and mine and for vivifying rice plants. In return the Malay magician let Islam affect his pretensions and his technique. It led him often to try to emulate the living Muslim saint, to whom folk resort for advice in legal disputes or as to the issue of any enterprise or as intercessor for the sick or to get a child or remove blight on crops or confound enemies. For his former Hindu practice of seclusion for certain days of the week or for a period, the magician now claimed an Arabic name (*khal-*

72

wat) and Islamic sanction. If he remained celibate or if he fasted to impress his clients or to enable himself to see visions, he was no longer a Hindu ascetic but the disciple of a crude Sufism also derived from India. Originally to become a shaman he had kept vigil beside an open grave or waited in the dark forest for the coming of a tiger familiar; he would now sit fasting and shrouded to hear the prayers for the dead read over him and he would repeat the name of Allah 5,000 times until hysteria brought nightmare visions of tiger or serpent to be succeeded by visions of angels and saints instructing him in mystic knowledge. The teaching of his shaman and Saiva forerunners made it natural for the Malay to accept the Sufi doctrine that a disciple must honour and obey his master and pass through several stages of initiation. And Brahmanical *mantra*, to which even the gods are subject, had prepared his mind for the audacities of the Indian Sufi, so that the pantheist magician could even ignore the terrific appearance of the archangels for the orthodox and cry:

> *I attest there is no God but Allah!*
> *I attest that Muhammad is His Prophet!*
> *Ho! my brethren Jibra'il, Mika'il, Israfil and 'Azra'il!*
> *Ye are four but with me five!*
> *I sit on the seat of Allah;*
> *I lean against the pillar of his throne;*
> *I use the pillar of the Ka'abah as my prop.*

One wonders if this is not a literal and erroneous interpretation by the Malay of al-Jili's description of the Perfect Man—'his heart stands over against the Throne of God ... He stands over against the angels with his good thoughts ... To every type of existence he furnishes from himself an antitype.' Unthinking hyperbole is certainly not the explanation of the cry of the Malay magician when about to plant the posts of his fishing-stakes, the cry that the posts lean against the pillar of God's Throne, that Allah hands them down and Muhammad receives them. It was a serious Persian mystic, Mansur Hallaj, who would say to one man 'Thou art Noah', to another 'Thou art Moses' and to a third, 'Thou art Muhammad', adding, 'I have caused their spirits to return to your bodies'.

Sufi speculations on the Perfect Man have been quaintly joined with Hindu imagery in an old Perak incantation for acquiring a dominant personality:

> I sit beneath the throne of Allah!
> Muhammad my shelter is beside me,
> Jibra'il on my right, Mika'il on my left,
> All the company of angels behind me
> Vicegerent of Allah . . .
> Only if Allah suffer harm,
> Can I suffer harm,
> Only if His Prophet suffer harm,
> Can I suffer harm.
> A hooded snake is my loin-cloth,
> A musty elephant my steed,
> My ear-posy the lightning,
> My shadow that of a fierce tiger.
> By virtue of this spell of Awang the Pre-eminent,
> In seated assembly pre-eminint I,
> Erect or walking or talking pre-eminent I,
> I lord of all mortals,
> Precious stone of the Prophet
> Pearl of God.

One is reminded of the Hermetic discourse known by the name of Poimandres, wherein the initiated possessor of the mysteries claims complete knowledge of the name and nature of God and complete equality with Him and addresses Him—'if anything happens to me this year, this month, this day or this hour, it will happen to the Great

A MAGICIAN'S FISHERMAN CLIENT

[*To face p.* 74

God also'. To the orthodox the claim of the magician that he is God or that he is the brother of the four Archangels seems hideous blasphemy, a claim allied with the blackest magic of the spirit-raising shaman. But to his disciple the exponent of this crude pantheism explains his attitude by many far-fetched analogies. Incantations used by a Kelantan magician are full of them. He calls, for example, upon four winds of disease to quit a patient's body by the four doors of the organs of the mystical life. Wind in skin and pores corresponds with the first of the four steps towards union with Allah, that is, with the observance of the law (*shari'at*), which is the outward mark of the religious and about which there is no secrecy. Wind in bone and sinew corresponds with the second stage, that is, the mystic path (*tarikat*) enjoined by his spiritual guide for the Sufi novice. Wind in flesh and blood corresponds with the third stage, the plane of truth (*hakikat*). Wind in the breath of life and the seed of man corresponds with the plane of perfect gnosis (*ma'rifat*). The process of thought is clear. The archangels are four; the first Caliphs were four; the elements out of which the body is composed are four; the limbs of the body are four. Therefore man and the Archangels are one![1] Adam, Muhammad and Allah can each be spelt in Arabic with four letters. Therefore Allah and man are identical. Such mysticism, wrote Snouck Hurgronje, 'is found also in Arabian lands but only in small circles of the initiated as half-secret doctrines of the Sufis, cautiously

[1] Other mystic numbers are three, founded on Sufi speculations on the trinity of the lover, the beloved and love, and seven, the number of stages in the Neo-Platonic theory of the emanation process of being, exemplified also in the number of the Pleiades and the days of the week. Twelve is a perfect number. The signs of the Zodiac and the months of the year are twelve; there were twelve great Patriarchs, twelve tribes of Israel, twelve Apostles of Christ, twelve Imams of the Shi'ahs. The Malay mystic might say with Verhaeren, 'Je suis l'hallucine de la forêt des Nombres.'

concealed on account of the hunt of official theologians for heresy and of the suspicious fanaticism of the vulgar. In the East Indies, however, it formed woof and warp not only of learned speculation but of popular belief.'

Obviously the identity of frail man with an all-powerful God was a dangerous creed. An eighteenth-century Perak charm-book contains a tremendous spell to be recited over seven blossoms that must then be handed to the object of one's passion: 'There is no God but God! *I* am God, the Divine Reality who blesseth all the worlds. There is no God but God, the King, the Revealed. There is no God but Allah, Lord of the heavens and the earth and of the great Throne.' Half a century ago a Perak man was sentenced to gaol for teaching an obscene form of pantheism that degraded the famous cry of Abu Sa'id, 'There is nothing inside this coat except Allah'. And there have been magicians of the baser sort ready to purvey spells (inherited from the Hindu) for the seduction of women; if the efficacy of an appeal to Allah and His Prophet for such an end was doubtful, then the assistance of the devil was invoked in a fashion patently impious:

> *In the name of Allah, the Merciful, the Compassionate.*
> *Friend of mine, Iblis! and all ye spirits and devils*
> *Who love to trouble man,*
> *I ask you to go and enter the body of this girl,*
> *Burning her heart as this sand burns,*
> *Fired with love for me.*
> *Bring her to yield herself to me!*
> *By virtue of this rice and steam*
> *Place her here by my hearth*
> *Or else take ye heed!*

Again. To destroy an enemy there is prescribed in Malay versions of Muslim treatises a world-wide method of sorcery. The pagan in Borneo makes a wooden image of his

76

enemy, immerses it in a pool of reddened water symbolical
of blood, transfixes it with a spear, buries it as those who
have died of violence are buried and invokes the hawk,
ominous messenger of the gods, to work his victim's death.
An Indian Muslim takes earth from a grave, kneads an
image of his enemy, and having read over it the 105th chapter of the Kuran strikes pegs into its trunk and limbs, wraps
it in cerements and buries it in a cemetery under the name
of his enemy. A Muslim Malay is advised to make an image
of wax from an empty honeycomb, pierce it with a skewer
from head to buttocks, shroud it and read over it the prayers
for the dead. Sometimes a cabalistic symbol is inscribed
on the wax.

Every good Malay Muslim views with horror this
Satanic magic.

Ordinarily, however, the magician had always employed
his lore for good ends, and now he claimed that his latest
knowledge was derived from a few scattered leaves of books
that belonged to the famous Lukman al-Hakim before at
Allah's command Gabriel upset him and his books at sea
as a punishment for his pride. In spite of his puerilities, an
example of Sufism from the Kelantan manuscript tract
already quoted (p. 75), a spell called 'The Fortress of
the Unity of God' will show that his lore was not without an intellectual and religious basis. The spell should be
recited four times a night from one Friday to the next 'with
a sincere vowing of the heart to unity with Allah and the
vision of Him implanted in one's heart, until His Being
permeates one and one has faith: "I am lost in the universal
and absolute Essence of God"; and one is lost to self and
one's self becomes absolute and universal too. Here it is:

'In the name of God, the Merciful, the Compassionate.
Oh God! grant peace to our lord Muhammad and the
household of Muhammad who watcheth over my self and
my friends and all my children and all the contents of my

77

house and my property and the possessions of my hands with a sevenfold fortress from the fortress of God Most High; its roof—"There is no God but God," and my wall "Muhammad the Apostle of God," and my key "the might of God", which may not be opened for ever save with His permission. Muhammad is like man and unlike man; he is like a chrysolite among stones.

'Now the meaning of the term "fortress" is that we know we come from not-being and to not-being shall return. For there is nothing evidently save the Being of God. And of a surety the Being of God never parts from His absolute essence, which carries out all His will, according to His word: 'His desire is accomplished by Himself and goes forth to no other than Himself save to not-being."

'The meaning of the term self is "spirit", one of the attributes of God Most High, which parts not from His essence and it becomes an individualized idea and is called man. Now the spirit is particularized and fettered. Always the spirit yearns towards God.

'The meaning of "the house" is the body. The body is the place of the spirit and so the veritable place that reveals God according to the saying of the Prophet, on whom be the peace of God: "Whosoever knows himself, knows his Lord." The house was built of itself and though it will pass away, yet He Whose house it is, is the Reality Who with His absolute essence is eternal.

'The meaning of our "property" is the liver and heart and lungs and gall and all that God Most High has created: according to His word: "There is no strength in any one save the strength of Allah, lord of all the worlds both as regards things revealed and things hidden."

'The meaning of our "possessions" is the ten senses, firstly the outward and secondly the inner. The outward are five: the sight of the eyes, the hearing of the ears, the taste of the tongue, the smelling of the nose, and the touch

78

of the hand. The inner also are five: desire, faith, consciousness, perception and judgment.

'The meaning of the sevenfold "fortress" is the creation by God Most High of man with seven attributes: life, knowledge, power, will, hearing, sight and speech. And seven parts of the body must be bowed to God in prayer: the forehead, the palms of the hands, the knees and the soles of the feet.

'The meaning of the "lock" is because we have utter trust and union by surrendering ourselves to God Most High, according to His word: "Hold yourselves fast to the cord of God which breaks not neither is there concealment of His will from mystical knowledge"; as said the Prophet on whom be God's peace:"Nothing at all moves save by permission of Allah." For we cannot behold aught if the cord break and it cannot break save by the will of God Most High, and there is no substitute for that cord.

'And the meaning of the "key" is Muhammad Apostle of God. For God is utterly hidden; none knoweth Him save in His own person. Therefore to cherish His glory, God Most High was revealed in the spirit of Muhammad our Prophet and from that spirit God Most High created all this universe, and all the attributes of His secret wisdom were revealed. So it is that Muhammad is called the "key", because he opened the treasure-house that was hidden, according to His word: "I opened that which was closed".

'And the meaning of the protection of God is according to His word: "God Most High is with thee wheresover thou art," according to His word: "God is nearer to thee than the muscles of thy neck."

'And the meaning of "roof" is the power of God to cover any of His servants with mercy according to His will, so that he be locked away from all enemies and danger in this world and the next, neither shall the lock be opened by genie or man save with the permission of God Most High.'

THE MALAY MAGICIAN

Was it to test the efficacy of some such charm as this that
that novice on the Sufi path, Sultan Ahmad of old Malacca, took his spiritual guide with him into battle against
the 'white Bengalis', descendants of genies, the first European invaders of Malaya?

X

MUSLIM MAGIC

ISLAM being brought to the Malay by Indian converts from Hinduism came moulded in a shape not utterly foreign to his past. For the first time he became the servant of One God, in Whose name one might banish spirits of evil, but so remote and august that the magician no more thought of Him in direct connection with the spirits that spoil crops and afflict villagers than the average European thinks of Him to-day in direct connection with bacteria or the tsetse fly. Besides, those spirits by the ingenuity of the Indian had had a place found for them along with Siva and the Hindu gods among a host of Islamic genies, whom it was still legitimate to invoke as supernatural creatures, although subservient to Allah. In fact, Islam not only tolerated the spirits and gods of older faiths but introduced the Malay to Iblis, a devil with whom his magic had never before had the chance of dealing. More important still, the magician was told of archangels, angels and saints, all of whom were benevolent to the righteous and innocent of the caprice of nature-spirits or of Siva, who was, it is true, creator but even more obviously destroyer. The new religion also brought new methods of divination and novel amulets and philtres. And finally in the pantheism of the Indian Muhammadan the Malay magician discovered analogies with his undying animism and fresh matter for his incantations.

(a) Animist and Muslim

It may well have been the pantheism of the Indian

81

Muhammadan which inspired a view held by Patani elders and midwives that 'all spirits are really one, pervading the whole world, only called by different names according to the environment in which the universal spirit of evil is considered for the moment. . . . As one old man expressed it, "It may be hot here and in Mecca at the same time and the spirit is the same". ' The whole idea of soul stuff impersonal and 'in widest commonalty spread' readily fitted into the pantheism of the Sufi, and syncretism was helped by fortuitous resemblance between old beliefs and new. For example, fresh sanction for spitting on the body of an infant (p. 109) was derived from the Muslim belief that the spittle of devout and learned men would endow a child with intelligence and ability to learn to recite the Kuran.

(b) Incantations

Islam changed the Sanskrit names (*mantra; jampi*) for spells into the Arabic word for prayer (*do'a*) and every one of them now ended with the Muslim confession of faith. The Sanskrit term *siddhi* 'may this be efficacious' was replaced by Arabic words of power. To ensure that the baited hook should catch in a crocodile's gullet, the Malay clenched his teeth and recited without drawing breath: ' "Let it be (*Kun*)," saith Allah. "And it is so (*Fayakunu*)" saith the Prophet. Fixed be this nail.' That for the control of spirit or beast there must be complete knowledge of their origin was an idea the Malay magician had got from the Hindu, but now he was compelled for that purpose to add and adapt the mythology of Islam to Indian mythology. Being regarded as the Malayan lion, the tiger, once an avatar of Siva, became associated with the Lion of God, 'Ali, the Prophet's son-in-law; and the crocodile, also an avatar of Siva, was therefore associated with 'Ali's wife, Fatimah, her plaything that had miraculously come to life.

MUSLIM MAGIC

I know thy origin!
From Fatimah thou art sprung!
Moulded from a clod of clay
Thy bones of sugar-cane knots!
Thy breast of palm-spathe.

There was much Shiʿah heresy in the doctrines of Islam as first imported from India and many Malay incantations are addressed to the Shiʿah hero, ʿAli, whose battle-cry so startled the cashew that ever since the nut has grown outside the fruit!

For now the magician's repertory of spells was greatly enlarged, the new not ousting but supplementing the old. Typical are some Muslim love-charms. A woman desiring the love of a man is advised to wrap a written spell in cerements that have covered the face of a male corpse and bury it where the object of her affections is bound to step. The spell runs:

If Muhammad can be sundered from Allah
And a corpse move in the grave,
Only then shall my lover's desire move to another.
The desire of his heart shall be only for me;
Straying nowhither he shall be my mate until death
Safe near me like a corpse in the grave.

So, a Moroccan bride will pray to Allah and the Prophet and Fatimah that her husband may 'be fond of her as the dead is fond of his grave'; and Syro-Christian charms that appear to have influenced early Islam invoke the Father and the Son to bind the tongues of false witnesses and the navel of the newly-born child as 'the ox in the yoke, the dead in the grave'.

Another Malay love-charm runs:

In the name of God, the Merciful, the Compassionate!
I fry sand from the footprint of my beloved;

83

Nay, I fry her heart and liver
Night and day, as this sand is fried.
'Let it be,' says Allah.
'And it is so,' says Muhammad, His Prophet.
Let her body itch with desire
Giving her no rest from longing for me.
'And it is so,' says Gabriel.

In exactly similar fashion the Hebrew sorcerer cries: 'Ye holy powerful angels! Just as this pot is burnt in the fire, so shall ye burn in the heart of so and so to follow after this girl.'

Finally, like Malay animism, so the Malay incantation became infected with pantheism. Some examples are accompanied by Yogi practices, designed to help the suppliant participate in the Islamic Logos for his personal safety. One such specimen instructs him that 'to marry body and spirit' he must draw all his breath into his heart and recite the following: 'I am the true Muhammad. It is not I that say it. It is Muhammad. First spirit was created and then the body. Only if this night be destroyed, can I be destroyed. My being is Thy being! My being is one with Thy being. I vanish in the fold of the attestation that "There is no God but Allah—Huwa!", in the fold of my mother, the Light of Muhammad until dawn.' If the spell is for protection by day, then it entrusts the reciter to the fold of his 'father, the Light of Muhammad'.

Equally blasphemous to the orthodox is the Muslim spell closing the old Tantric ritual by which the Kelantan shaman exorcizes a spirit at a *séance* for the sick:

O universe, the world of Adam!
Earth was made from a clod from Paradise;
Water from a river of Paradise;
Fire from the smoke of Hell;
Air from the four elements.

Skin and hair, flesh and blood,
Bones and sinews, life and seed
Come from the four elements of sperm.
Skin and hair were created by Jibra'il,
Flesh and blood by Mika'il,
Bones and sinews by Israfil,
Life and seed by 'Azra'il!
Where are you genies lodging and lurking?
Where are you lodging and crouching?
Genies! if ye are in the feet of this patient,
Know that by these feet walk Allah and His Prophet;
If ye are in the belly of this patient,
His belly is God's sea, the sea too of Muhammad;
If ye are in his hands,
Those hands are hands that pay homage to Allah and His
*   Prophet;*
If ye are in his liver,
His liver is the secret place of Allah and His Prophet;
If ye are in his heart,
His heart is the palace of Abubakar;
If ye are in his lungs,
His lungs are 'Omar's palace;
If ye are in his spleen,
His spleen is 'Uthman's palace;
If ye are in his gall-bladder:
His gall-bladder is 'Ali's palace.
Heart, lungs, spleen and gall-bladder
Are the homestead of life,
Not of genies, devils, sickness and suffering.
Ho, there, genies! ye are sprung from the tongue-like fumes of
*   smokeless hell.*

In man, the microcosm, the Malay's latest faith found equivalents for all that is both in the spiritual and material worlds; his backbone corresponds to the pillar of God's

85

throne (the *primum mobile*), his bile to fire, his phlegm to water, his blood to air, his belly to the ocean, his spirit to a bird. Hence the terms of exorcism employed by the Kelantan medicine-man.

(c) Sacrifice

Islam also introduced new ideas about sacrifice. A Kelantan magician will put dough images of birds, beasts and fishes on a tray, make the patient hold a parti-coloured thread, one end of which is stuck under a taper, and recite an incantation commanding the spirits that have caused the sickness to accept the banquet of flesh and blood, sharks, lobsters, and crabs, the various kinds of substitute laid out on the tray. The use of parti-coloured thread certainly came from Mesopotamian wizardry. And dough is foreign to a rice-eating people.

A type of sacrificial offering that clearly had no particular significance before the coming of Islam is the offering of pork and spirituous liquor. In dire illness Muslim Arabs will use pork as medicine and if other offerings have failed to bring catches to the Kelantan fishermen, the pious depart and a pig is sacrificed on the seashore. In a ceremony at Selangor fishing-stakes arrack was offered by the Muslim celebrant to the gods of the sea.

Sometimes Muhammadanism lent old-world sacrifice the sanction of Arabian precedent. In the foundations of a new house, the Indonesian Dayak, untouched by Muslim influence, placed formerly a slave-girl and more recently a fowl to be crushed to death, and he sprinkled the pillars with the victim's blood. The Malay of the Peninsula slits in orthodox fashion the throat of fowl, goat or buffalo, according to his means and the degree of malignity imputed to the local earth-spirits; sometimes he bids the vengeful children of Siva avaunt, sometimes he recites

Muslim prayers and calls on Allah and His Prophet. Sacrifice at the laying of a foundation popular Islam could not condemn. For so too Arabs offer a victim on the threshold of a new building to placate genies jealous of the trespass.

(d) Divination

Islam not only affected the Malay spell and added to the types of Malay sacrifice. It led also to employment of foreign types of divination, and new kinds of amulet and to borrowing from the Gnostics a magical use of names and formulae.

In the Hindu table of the Five Ominous Times (p. 32) the Malay substituted for the names of the Hindu deities the names Ahmad, Jibra'il, Ibrahim, Yusuf and 'Azra'il. One Muslim planetary system employed by Malays for astrological divination placed the sun midway between the superior planets, Saturn, Jupiter, Mars, and the inferior planets, Venus, Mercury and the Moon. Under this system, that came in with Copernican astronomy, every hour of the day was assigned to one planet. Since the Egyptian day began at sunrise, the first hour of the first day of the month was under the influence of Shams, the sun, subsequent hours being under Kamar the moon, Marikh (Mars), 'Utarid (Mercury), Mushtari (Jupiter), Zaharat (Venus) and Zahal (Saturn). Because the twenty-four hours are not divisible by seven but have three over, the first hour of the next day is dedicated to the third planet after Shams, namely the moon, and so on, so that we get the order familiar in our week, Sunday, Monday, etc. Work done in the hour of the sun Malay astrology says will succeed: a moon hour should be spent in study or hunting or fishing; hours assigned to Mars are inauspicious for all work; under Mercury men are hot; Jupiter's hours are auspicious for study, healing quarrels and writing spells in saffron ink; hours assigned to Venus are good for marriage and planting; Saturn's hours are inauspicious for work but good for hunting and success in quarrels. There is also a Malay system of divination from the signs of the Zodiac. The Muslim element in Malay magic brought many crude astrological devices to determine lucky and unlucky days for begetting children, going to war, planting, building a house. At the Perak court the moment propitious for the circumcision of a prince was divined from pools of oil floating on water 'in the shape of moon and stars', a method employed as early as when Hammurabi was king of Babylon. There are amulets that must be inscribed only when the constellation Scorpion is invisible. There are several ways of discovering how long one will live, ways different according to the month of the Muhammadan year. In the first month one has to close one's eyes at midnight, recite, 'Say, "God is one",' ten times and then open one's eyes and gaze at the moon: if it looks black, one will die. In the fifth and sixth months one must gaze not at the moon but at a lamp and that only on a Wednesday night. In other months, one gazes at water in a bowl or at a cloudless sky; if they look red, one will die.

A legacy from Yogi ritual was a number of ways of divination by observing the breath. Crude mysticism found seats for the four Caliphs in the human frame. Abu-Bakar, for example, passed to his seat in the liver up the nostrils. So, if one wanted to cross a river without a boat, one could consult Abu-Bakar by inhaling and exhaling. A heavy sensation betokened water too deep for wading; a light sensation shallowness.

There is a Malay treatise called the *Crown of Kings* (*Taj-al-Mulk*) of which several editions have been printed in Egypt and at Mecca. Its author was an Achehnese, prominent in war against the Dutch, Shaikh 'Abbas, who died in 1895. The book is interesting because, like 'the majority of

88

Muslim philosophers and authors of bibliographical and encyclopaedic works', the compiler 'keeping to the classification of the sciences given by the Aristotelians, considers astrology as one of the seven or nine branches of the natural sciences, placing it with medicine, physiognomy, alchemy, the interpretation of dreams and so on'. The tract is a fair example of what Islam taught the Malay to regard as science, and it is, in effect, a repertory of his latest magical lore. The author begins by saying that astrology as first taught by Enoch was simple and that it became complex and difficult only at the prayer of Jesus, whose whereabouts before His arrest by the Jews were betrayed by astrological computations. Among his authorities he quotes Abu Ma'shar, an Arab astrologer known to Christendom in the Middle Ages as Albumasar, and he quotes Ja'far al-Sadik, the sixth of the twelve Imams and reputed by the Shi'ahs to have been the author of a book of infallible astrological prognostications for the information of the House of the Prophet. Versions of these prognostications exist in Malay, Javanese and Achehnese.

Astrology does not enter into all branches of divination. A Kelantan warrior would invoke thrice the four Shaikhs at the corners of the world, the four first Caliphs of Islam, the four archangels, the blessed saints, all miracle-working rulers dead and alive and pray them to intercede with God to reveal the issue of a coming battle. Then he gazed at his followers. If he saw them headless, they would perish: if armless, they would suffer greatly in the fight. Or he might listen three times. If he heard no sound, his men would perish.

A Kelantan magician, whose lore was full of Muslim borrowings, claimed that for the purpose of divination he could reflect genies on the finger-nails of innocent little boys. And Sir Frank Swettenham met an Arab in Malaya who declared that he could see a robbery re-enacted on the surface of water, but that first of all he would see a little old genie by whose help the scene of the crime would be reflected. Sir Frank also saw a bowl of water, with a cotton cloth tied taut across it, used as a *planchette* to discover a thief. A chapter of the Kuran was read, two men supported the bowl by the rim, and when at last a paper inscribed with the name of one of the suspects was laid on the lid, the bowl began to revolve. The bowl failed to respond to four previous names; the names were written in English characters unintelligible to the Malays present and the experiment succeeded twice. Among the regalia of the ruler of Negri Sembilan is a bowl and a hair, a very ancient apparatus for the discovery of a thief. The bowl is divided by lines of Indian ink into eight compartments, each inscribed with the name of a suspect and with Kuranic texts. A blind man holds the hair, to which a gold ring is tied, above the centre of the bowl and intones a Muslim prayer, whereupon if the name of the culprit is there, the ring swings violently into the compartment containing it. The hair should be from a maiden's head. The Prophet, be it noted, condemned divination. According to Abu Mas'ud al-Ansari, he declared unlawful the price of a dog, the wages of immorality, and the fee of a diviner. According to 'Aisha he explained that the angels descend in rain-clouds and mention what has been decreed in heaven, while genies listen and repeat their words to diviners who add a hundred lies out of their own minds. But even in Arabia his words were unheeded.

All Malay treatises on divination from dreams bear an Arabic title and are of Muslim origin. A popular poem on the subject begins by explaining the omens to be drawn from dreaming that one sees Allah, meets an angel, beholds the Throne of God or Paradise or the Razor Bridge across hell-fire or the Guarded Tablet of Fate. Then it interprets the meaning of dreams about the Four Friends of Muhammad, the Kuran, Iblis, being banished by a Shaikh, riding a camel, seeing a date palm or a fig tree. All such manuals are divided into the class of object about which one dreams: men, beasts, flora, clothes, birds, insects, fruits, musical instruments and traps for fish and game. None of their theology, zoology or botany is Malay.

There are Malay translations of tracts that enumerate many animals, pigs, the rhinoceros, wild dogs, deer, whose entrance into a garden forebodes calamity, unless the evil portent is averted by prayers and by the gift of cash, cloth, and a feast to the pious who recite them. ' "Taking a bad omen is polytheism." These words Muhammad repeated thrice. "There is not one of us but will have evil presentiments removed by God if he trust in Him." ' That saying popular superstition has construed literally. Butterflies, bees, hawks, woodpeckers alighting on a roof, frogs, monkeys, snakes and geckoes invading house or garden, a tortoise under the floor, fungus growing in a kitchen, coconuts two on a stem, nests of wasps or mason-bees in one's clothes—all these accidents of circumstance portend variously poverty, divorce, disease or death, disasters which the recital of an appropriate passage from the Kuran can change into riches, health and happiness. When a mat belonging to the second Abbaside Caliph was gnawed by a mouse, a diviner interpreted it to portend a quiet and prosperous reign for its owner. The Malay manuscript from which a list of ominous visitants has just been quoted concludes with a dissertation on the omens to be drawn from the gnawing by mice of mats or pillows or of the neck, right arm or left arm or bottom or side or back of a man's coat!

The *Crown of Kings* devoted several pages to the omens to be drawn from involuntary convulsive movements of the left eyebrow, the right eyelid, the left nostril, the upper lip, the shoulder-blades, the left ring-finger and every part of the body. The romantic story of Hang Tuah makes that hero of mediaeval Malacca wear his magic creese one day because an involuntary twitch of his right shoulder led him to expect a brawl. But few modern Malays have studied these intimations or pay heed to them.

Divination by the values attached to the letters of men's names is best known from a 'Poem on Affinities': the Arabic *abjad* or alphabet of letters representing numerical values is employed.

Arab diviners, the interpretation of omens on Arabic lines, the adoption of the Arabic system of astrology, the employment of texts from the Kuran all show that the forms of divination popular among Malays in recent times have been derived from Muslim sources. Muslim superstition has entered even into the daily life of the Malay. One of the Traditions records that the Prophet forbade Muslims to drink standing, just as Brahmin students are forbidden. And this prohibition is commonly observed by Malay villagers, who are ignorant of the other Tradition that Muhammad used to drink standing, and of Ibn Kutaiba's effort to reconcile these conflicting accounts of the Prophet's views and practice.

(e) Amulets and philtres

In place of the animist's fetish Islam gave the Malay the amulet inscribed with magic squares, cabalistic letters, the signs of the planets or the signs of the Zodiac, the names of the angels and the Excellent Names of Allah. The Prophet is related to have countenanced the wearing of amulets against the evil eye, for snake-bites and against some diseases, but he held that 'He who depends on a thing will be left trusting to it' and himself relied on prayer. Mu'awiya, the son of al-Hakam, once said to him, 'In the days of ignorance we drew lines', and Muhammad answered, 'One of the Prophets drew lines and he whose drawing accords with his is right'. With this qualified sanction the hexagonal star of Solomon's seal is employed by Malays to cure madness and possession by devil, genie or ghost. In Perak paper inscribed with three such stars is steeped in water for washing the face of one afflicted with dizziness. A magic square scratched on leaf or paper and buried in a rice-field will keep rats and pests away from the plants. Arabic characters for K, M, Y, D, Z, ALA, if traced in oil on the palm of the hand and rubbed furtively on one's face in the presence of one of the opposite sex, will attract that person's love. Another such formula will bring the fisherman a good catch. Yet another put under the pillow will induce sleep. An appropriate text from the Kuran hung on one's person will avert convulsions or cure an aching limb. The school-boy will write a text on paper, dip it in water and drink the water in order to command divine aid in the examination room.

There is a translation by a Kelantan Malay of a treatise popular with Indian Sunnis, the *Mujarrabat-i-Dirbi* or 'Prescriptions', which cites among its sources works by al-Buni, a celebrated Arabian writer on the Kabbala, divination and magic squares. In one passage al-Buni extols the virtues of the *Basmala*—the Arabic formula for the words 'In the name of Allah, the Merciful, the Compassionate'. 'When God sent down the *Basmala*,' he writes, 'the hills shook. Its Arabic letters are nineteen, the number of the angels in charge of hell; whosoever recites them shall not be damned. It was the *Basmala* that set up Solomon's kingdom. Whoever writes it down six hundred times and wears it shall be honoured by men. Whoever recites it seven hundred and eighty-six times for seven consecutive days shall gain whatever he desires. Read fifty times over the face of a tyrant it will bring him low. Written down sixty-one times and worn it will make the barren fruitful. Written on tin and put in a fishing-net it will attract shoals from all the seas.'

As well as amulets, many philtres were imported with Islam. According to an old Hebrew prescription, the burnt ashes of a black kitten will enable one to see demons, and 'the ashes of a black cat are a popular form of magicians' stock-in-trade in modern Arabic books on sorcery'. The Kelantan magician saturates seven pieces of thread in the blood of a murdered man and the blood of a buffalo, adds the eyes of a tiger and the eyes of a black cat, burns all these ingredients to ashes, mixes the ashes with oil and rubs the philtre on his eyebrows to enable him to see through a dice-box. Yet to the Malay as to the Hindu it was sinful to kill a cat. Indeed he believes that, if he kills a cat, in the next world he will have to carry and pile logs of wood as big as coconut palms and as many as the hairs on the beast's body.

The contribution of Islam to Malay magic is hardly interesting. Flotsam and jetsam from the Talmud, the works of the Gnostics, the science of Indian astrologers and the practices of Indian sorcerers who had embraced the religion of the Prophet, it came to the Malay world third-hand. Of what Christians term the Gnostic heresy, it has been well said that 'it was specially dangerous from the prevalence in it of the conviction that by the magical use of mystic names and formulae the soul could secure its own salvation and, as it were, take the kingdom of God by storm.'

(f) Angels and Devils of Islam

To-day in every hamlet in Malaya, that has sufficient inhabitants to form a congregation, there is a mosque where, along with his fellow villagers, the magician acknowledges that there is no God but Allah and Muhammad is His Prophet. The office of Caliph or head of the Muslim faith within his own state is the most cherished prerogative of a Malay ruler. His installation is attended by the magician, once master of the ceremony but now merely an onlooker, who sees court officials conduct a Hindu ritual and hears the Muslim authorities call to the four archangels to send down upon their new ruler 'the divine majesty of kings by the hands of his angels: the angels of the rising sun, the angels of the evening, the angels who stand upon the right and left of the empyrean throne, the angel of the zenith and the horned princess, angel of the moon.' Suckled in creeds outworn, the magician has sat for centuries at the feet of the pious and learnt all he can about these angels and the demonology of the youngest of Malaya's religions. He has added the names of Muslim angels and devils and spirits to his repertory of incantations.

He has learnt that there are angels, demons (or Shaitan) and jinn, all higher than man. Actually he has had a Malay account of Muhammadan mythology for nearly three hundred years in a work called the *Garden of Kings*, written in A.D. 1638 by an Indian missionary of Islam in Acheen. That work tells him of the four angels who bear the throne of God, one in the form of a bull, one in the form of a tiger, one in the form of an eagle, and one in the form of a man. It tells also of the cherubim who cry incessantly 'Glory to God'. But more interesting to him are the four archangels with individual names, who are concerned with the welfare of men. There is Jibra'il, the angel of revelation, with six pinions, each composed of one hundred smaller wings; he is covered with saffron hairs; between his eyes is a sun, and between every two hairs of his body a moon and stars. Every day he dives three hundred and sixty times into the Sea of Light, and every drop of water from his wings creates a spiritual angel (*Ruhaniyun*) in his likeness. Two of his pinions he expands only when God desires to destroy hamlet or town. Two green pinions he opens only once annually on the night of destiny, when from the tree that stands by the throne of God the leaves fall inscribed with the names of those who shall die during the ensuing year.

There is Mika'il, created five hundred years before Gabriel and five hundred years after Israfil. His whole body is covered with saffron hairs, every hair possessing a million faces having a thousand mouths, each mouth containing a thousand tongues that entreat the mercy of God, while the tears of his million eyes, weeping for the sins of the faithful, create cherubim in his likeness. These cherubim are his servants, who control rain and plants and fruits, so that there is not a drop of rain falling on earth or sea that is not watched by one of them. There is Israfil, whose head is level with the throne of Allah and whose feet reach lower than the lowest earth. With one pinion he envelopes the west, with another the east; with a third he covers his person, and with a fourth he veils himself from mouth to chest. Between his eyes is the jewelled tablet of fate. His duty it will be to sound the last trump on the day of judgment. There is 'Azra'il, who according to this version is not (as he should be) the angel of death but only his warder, and is like Israfil in appearance. The angel of death, bigger than the seven earths and the seven heavens, God kept hidden and chained with seventy thousand chains until the creation of Adam. When he was seen by the angels, they fell into a faint that lasted a thousand years. He has seven thousand pinions. His body is full of eyes and tongues, as many as there are men and birds and living things. Whenever a mortal dies, an eye closes. He has four faces. When he takes the life of prophet or angel, he shows the face on his head; the face on his chest is shown to believers, the face on his back to infidels, and the face on the soles of two of his feet to jinn. Of his other two feet one is on the borders of heaven, the other on the brink of hell. So huge is he that if the waters of all seas and all rivers were poured upon his head, not one drop would reach the earth. No living creature shall escape death except the four archangels and the four angels who bear the throne of God.

There is also a huge angel called Ruh or the Spirit, with the face of a man, who will stand beside the throne on the day of judgment and implore mercy for the faithful.

There are the two inquisitor angels, Munkar and Nakir, who visit the dead in their graves and inquire if they are believers.

Night and day man is protected from devils and jinn by two out of four attendant angels, who change guard at sunrise and sunset, so that particularly at these hours he is exposed to danger, a Muslim belief that aptly fitted the primitive Malay dread of sunset. Recorders of his good and evil deeds, these angels are termed Kiraman Katibin, the Noble Writers; good deeds are written down by the angel on his right, bad by the angel on his left.

Nineteen Zabaniah (or Guardian Angels), under Malik their chief, are in charge of hell.

Finally, Iblis, the fallen rebel angel who refused to prostrate himself before Adam, is commander of an army of supreme interest to the magician, the host of infidel genies or jinn.

(g) Muslim Genies

Islam, tolerant as Christianity over earlier beliefs, allowed the Malay to retain the nature-spirits of the animist and even the gods of the Hindu under the orthodox designation of infidel genies or jinn or (in Dutch spelling) djinn, the spirits and goblins of Arabia's pagan days.

The origin of these latest arrivals in his ghostly pantheon was for the Malay magician a matter of great moment if he was to command them. So not content with the statement in the Kuran that they were created from smokeless fire, he groped among animistic beliefs and Hindu and Arabian myth for clues to their pedigree. For the Malay has always been as interested as any evolutionist in tracing a relation between his successive beliefs.

97

Arab myth asserts that Jan, a serpent from over the sea, was the father of all genies. But for the Malay cradled in Hindu mythology Saktimuna was the greatest serpent from over the sea. Therefore Saktimuna must have been another name for the jinns' progenitor Jan, who created the king of the jinn from his life's breath, white jinn from the white of his eyes, black, blue, green and yellow jinn from their irises, the genie that lives in the lightning from his voice. Again, Iblis, the devil, according to another Arabian myth, was the ancestor of all jinn. But Siva, as chief of the Malay's heathen gods, must have been the chief of Islam's devils; so Siva as Kala the black god of death is also credited with being the father of all genies. Or according to one incantation, they were created from the earth of Mount Mahameru, the Hindu Olympus, probably because the Arabs put their main abode on the mythical mountain range of Kaf. The old-fashioned Malay was quite happy 'voyaging through strange seas of thought alone' with an eye blind to language frontiers, inconsistencies and the lapse of centuries. One Malay incantation speaks of jinn the children of Jan of the line of the Pharaohs, a pedigree founded on the Arab notion that the last king of the pre-Adamite jinn was Jan the son of Jan and that he built the Pyramids. Another incantation talks of the genie who is lord of death, son of the prince of plague, grandson of Pharaoh. Another myth relates that Cain and Abel while still in the womb bit their thumbs till the blood came and that along with them were born genies, black from the blood that spouted sky-high, white from the blood that dripped on the ground. This variety of Arabian myth fired the fancy of the Malay magician. Regardless of the pedigree he had established for them, sometimes his incantations address genies as born of the afterbirth, sometimes as offspring of the morning star. Yet another Malay account derives their origin from three mangrove-leaves, the green genies from a leaf that soared

into the green sky, the black from a leaf that fell at the gate
of the forest, the white from a leaf that fell into the sea.

One of the earliest, if not the earliest, picture of jinn that
reached the Malay is to be found in his version of the story
of Alexander the Great, as a missionary of Islam. That
world-conqueror meets a descendant of the genie Sakhr,
who stole Solomon's ring and assuming Solomon's shape
reigned in his stead for forty days. He and his kin are
guarding till the day of judgment a mosque built for Solomon by Sakhr in retribution for his presumption. He appears
to Alexander in the form of a handsome youth but turns
by request into his proper shape, huge as a mosque, having
seven heads, each with two faces, each face having four
eyes like tongues of flame, a cavernous mouth, teeth like
fiery tongues, a nose like the nose of a bull: on each forehead are two snakey locks, and the genie has the feet of a
duck and the tail of a bull! Near the border of the world
where the sun sinks Alexander finds genies, descendants of
men and the ten daughters of Iblis, guarding King Solomon's treasure-house of jewels. When Alexander marvels,
the Prophet Khidzr tells him of the queen of Sheba who
had a human father and a genie mother and whose origin
Solomon detected from the hair on her calves. For all jinn
are the subjects of Solomon, to whom Allah gave authority
over them and the animal creation and the wind of heaven. In
the story of the fisherman in the Arabian Nights, the genie is
confined in a vase sealed with Solomon's ring, which bears
the sign of the six-pointed star that is a potent Malay talisman.

Again. For more than three hundred years the Malay has
read of genies in the *Bustan al-Salathin* or 'Garden of Kings'.
Jan their father, he is told, was originally an angel, called
firstly Aristotle but later 'Azazil. When 'Azazil refused to
do obeisance to Adam, his name was changed to Iblis[1] or

---

[1] Some say that Iblis and his wife Marijah were the parents not of
Muslim genies but of the devils, and that Jan was a different creature from
Iblis.

Jan and his form into that of a genie. Begetting a child every two days, Jan became the ancestor of all the jinn, countless shadowy beings, numerous as the sands of the earth and filling mountain and plain, forest and cave. At first they inhabited the lowest heaven. Thence they got Allah's permission to descend to earth, seven thousand troops of them. In time they fought among themselves and disobeyed Allah. So He sent Prophets and Angels to quell them and pen them in a corner of the world. To plague mankind, genies can assume any shape. Some take the form of men, others of horses or dogs or pigs, others of snakes, others of insects. Some can fly. Some can eat, drink and marry. One tradition talks of three classes of jinn, one winged, another in the form of dogs and insects, another in human form. A few are good Muslims who listened to the teaching of Muhammad and will go to heaven; most are infidels doomed to hell. Their great age is illustrated from the story of the genie detected by Muhammad under the disguise of a very old man. Being recognized as a genie, he admitted that he had met Noah and all the prophets after him. Like angels and men, all genies are mortal in the end.

According to Malay belief the colour of a genie varies according to his habitation. Genies of the earth and dark forests and lowering clouds are black. Those inhabiting the sky are green. In fleecy clouds and the shimmering sea they are white. The genies of fire and sunset are yellow. For though one tradition of the Prophet distinguishes three kinds of genies, one in the air, one on land and one on sea, Malay medical lore having learnt of Plato's theory of the origin of disease, differentiates a fourth class, the genies of fire and fiery sunsets, and so completes the tale,

'of those demons that are found
In fire, air, flood or underground,

MUSLIM MAGIC

Whose power hath a true consent
With planet or with element.'

Just as Plato ascribed disease to disturbance of the balance of
power between the four properties of earth, air, fire and
water, out of which the body is compacted, so the Malay
medicine-man ascribes all diseases to the four classes of jinn
presiding over those properties. The genies of the air cause
wind-borne complaints, dropsy, blindness, hemiplegia and
insanity. The genies of the black earth cause vertigo with
sudden blackness of vision. The genies of fire cause hot
fevers and yellow jaundice. The white genies of the sea
cause chills, catarrhs and agues.

All these jinn are visible to lonely wayfarers, to a
magician in his trance or, according to Kelantan belief, to
the gazer upon the finger-nails of innocent little boys. They
can talk among themselves or through the mouth of the
shaman medium. Genies of the earth may appear in human
form 'floating in the air and not always remaining the same
size', or in the form of animals or ants or scorpions or in any
shape they please. The manufacture of old Chinese crackle-
ware is ascribed to jinn. Muslim jinn haunt two mosques in
Negri Sembilan, flitting to and fro in long white robes and
sometimes chanting the Kuran. If a person stands under a
ladder and bathes in water wherein a corpse has been
washed, he has only to stoop and look between his legs to
see crowds of jinn and demons sipping the water. Infidel
genies of the earth are thought in Patani to assume the form
of dogs and guard hidden treasure. If they take a fancy to a
person, they change into little old men and leave sacks of
gold for their favourites to remove. Bubbles on the surface
of water indicate the presence of jars of treasure placed by
genies in pool or well. There is a genie in human form who
darts about like a will-o'-the-wisp and dazes the man that
crosses him. Seize a genie and hold him, no matter what

terrifying shape he may assume, and one can wrest from him riches or the secret of invisibility. 'If a man had a tame genie he could cause the meat of another man's cooking-pot to come to him.'

Malay fancy has found in some genies a local habitation and a name for abstract ideas.

> *The genie of golden life,*
> *The genie of bright desire,*
> *Wearing bangles of brass and coat of steel*

can both abduct a woman's soul on her lover's behalf. For while orthodox genies are moral beings, the others are capricious and do not distinguish between good and evil.

A Magician's Village

[To face p. 102

XI

MAGIC IN DAILY LIFE

To protect the soul-substance of his staple food-plant the Malay peasant, conservative as agriculturists all the world over, is content with the primitive ritual of the animist, covered for decency's sake with a thin veneer of his later religions. Courts and ports, where new faiths first found acceptance, are more open to foreign influences, and to safeguard the body and soul of man the Malay has added to the practices of the animist all the magic that Hindu and Muslim could teach him. Like all primitive peoples, he believes that evil spirits are especially active on the abnormal occasions of life, so that birth, puberty and marriage are invested with the most lavish ceremonial. For the dead he accepts Muhammadan rites almost unalloyed.

(a) Birth and Infancy

As soon as a Malay woman is with child, she and her husband have to observe certain rules and abstentions, so that no vampire may injure the expectant mother, no prenatal influence affect the unborn, and nothing impede or mar a safe delivery (p. 16).

To frustrate evil spirits the woman must carry a knife or iron of some sort as a talisman, whenever she ventures abroad. If her husband stir out of his house after dark, he may not return direct but must visit a neighbour's house first to put any chance vampire following him off the scent. At the time of an eclipse when spirits prowl, the woman must hide under the shelf in the kitchen, armed with a wooden spoon and wearing as a helmet of repulsion the rattan basket-stand that is used for the base purpose of supporting the round-bottomed cooking pots. Every Friday she must bathe with limes, a fruit distasteful to devils, and drink the water that drops off the ends of her tresses.

In Upper Perak another rite precedes the customary lustration in the seventh month of a first pregnancy. Apparently it is an example of imitative magic, designed to facilitate delivery. A palm-blossom is swathed to represent a baby with a child's brooch on the bosom. This doll, adorned with flowers, is laid on a tray and the tray placed in a cradle made of three, five or seven layers of cloth according to the rank of the prospective parents. Midwife and magician sprinkle rice-paste on doll and cradle. The midwife rocks the cradle, crooning baby songs. Then she gives the doll to the future mother and father and all their relatives to dandle. Finally the doll is put back into the cradle and left there till the next day, when it is broken up and thrown into water.

Everywhere when a woman has gone seven months with her first child there is performed a ceremony, observed also by Indian Muslims. In Malaya, to-day, it is begun with chants in praise of the Prophet. Next morning husband and wife, arrayed in holiday attire, are escorted down to the river. Incense is burnt. Toasted, saffron and white rice and a cooling rice-paste are sprinkled as at every momentous business of Malay life, at seed-time and harvest, at birth, at the shaving of a child's head, at circumcision, in sickness, on return from a long journey, at a chief's installation, at a warrior's preparation for battle. Now it is sprinkled on water for lustration. The couple are bathed, a white cloth is stretched above their heads, coconut palms are waved over them seven times, and they are drenched with water specially charmed to avert evil and procure well-being, as at the lustration after marriage. Two candles are lit and carried thrice about their heads, and they must face the light with direct glances to avoid any chance of their child being squint-eyed. Then the procession returns to the house, where the couple sit together in state as at a wedding. Shawls are spread on the floor (seven if the patient is a raja), and the expectant mother lies on her back with the shawls under her waist. The midwife seizes the ends of the first shawl and rocks the woman slowly as in a hammock, removes it, seizes the ends of the next shawl and repeats the performance seven times. Among the presents given to the midwife as her retaining fee on this occasion is a betel-tray. The contents of this she empties: if all of them drop together, it is a sign that delivery will be easy. In Negri Sembilan betel-nuts are cut into pieces and thrown like dice, inferences being drawn as to the sex of the unborn child according as more flat or rounded surfaces lie uppermost.

The magician 'chooses an auspicious place for the birth and surrounds it with thorns, nets, rays' tails, bees' nests, dolls, bitter herbs and a rattan cooking-pot stand, to keep the spirits of evil from molesting mother and child in the perilous hour of their weakness. He selects the suitable spot by dropping a chopper or axe-head and marking the place where it first sticks upright in the ground. Thorns and rays' tails are thought to be dangerous to the trailing entrails of the vampire; bitter herbs are unpalatable to every one; dolls may be mistaken for the baby; nets and bees' nests are puzzling to spirits because of their complexity, and sometimes a much-perforated coconut is hung over the door to bewilder ghosts by the multiplicity of its entrances and exits.' Most of these demon-traps are set under the floor of the house. But over the patient's head is hung a fisherman's net and a bunch of the red *Dracoena*, whose tough vital power denotes its strong soul-substance. By some midwives imitation weapons of lathe are suspended from the

H 105

roof. The midwife may dress as a man. All locks on door or box are opened, the sufferer's hair is unbound, and any knot in her clothes is untied.

If delivery is difficult, the magician may be called to lift the end of the woman's tresses and blow down them. Or he may recite charms or write a text from the Kuran on paper and tie it round waist or thigh, or the midwife will rub on her abdomen a mixture of rose-water and the dried gut and gall-bladder of a slow-eyed loris. The husband will be summoned to step to and fro across his wife or kiss her, thus condoning any sins she may have committed against him. If the woman is a raja, chiefs will make vows of a goat or other offering for her recovery. To register each vow, the midwife ties a ring round the wrist of the patient. Should the throes be prolonged, husband or mother puts dollars under the sufferer's back to be distributed in charity when her peril is past. According to a tradition Muhammad said, that a vow brings nothing to a son of man that has not been decreed for him, howbeit it precipitates him towards his destiny and extracts something from the avaricious.

If the afterbirth will not follow, a portion of the umbilical cord is cut from the child and tied to the patient's thigh as a kind of sympathetic attraction. A boy born with a caul is considered very lucky. Immediately after birth the umbilical cord is tied with seven circles of black fibre and severed with a bamboo knife: later, when the cord falls off, a poultice is applied, mixed with pepper to make the child brave. In Negri Sembilan it is believed that if the severed cords of a woman's successive children are preserved together, these children will not quarrel or be disunited when they grow up.

Her trouble over, the mother is laid on a platform and warmed frequently during forty-four days of seclusion. In various forms this primitive practice is widely spread; it survives in Hindu ritual with invocations to Agni and away in Siberia a Tungu woman jumps through fire for purification. As for seclusion, 'the contagion of woman during the sexual crises of menstruation, pregnancy, childbirth, is simply intensified, because these are occasions when woman's pecular characteristics are accentuated, these are feminine crises when a woman is most a woman'. The savage dreads the contagion of her effeminacy, weakness, timidity and hysteria. And survivals of this dread may be traced in the observance of continence by Malay warriors and fishermen, in the notion that menstrual blood can cause leprosy, in the custom of husband and wife feeding separately except on the occasion of their marriage.

A midwife spits on the child she welcomes into the world; this is a gift of a portion of herself, a pledge of union and good-will, a diluted form of blood-covenent.

A baby's first cradle is a tray on which are placed a bit of iron and a peck of unhusked rice. In Perak 'when the baby is promoted from this tray, the rice whereon he has lain is measured to foretell his future; if the measure is brimming, he will be rich; if it is short, poor; the balance of the rice is thrown to the chicken to avert ill-luck.'

A brush is dipped in a black mixture made of burnt coconut shell, and the eyebrows and outlines (*rajah*) of the nose, chin, and other features are marked in black so that demons may not recognize or desire the infant. A cross is put on the forehead and a spot on the nose. In Selangor a girl's forehead is marked with a cross, a boy's with a mark recalling the caste mark of the Hindu. The mother, also, is daubed on nose and bosom.

In some parts the moulding of the child's head, due to the process of birth, is reduced by massage or a constricting cap.

A tentative name is given to a child before the umbilical cord is cut. 'In Upper Perak names suggested by some local circumstances are given at birth, and girls, for example, are called after a butterfly, a fish, a plant. Later the parents will consult a religious elder to take a horoscope and select a Muhammadan name for the child according to the date of the birth'—a difficult task, because even a name like 'Abd al-Kadir may offend the saintly founder of the great religious order called after him. 'This name may be adopted temporarily or permanently. The original pagan name may be used still but will be changed for another in the event of sickness' to mislead the spirits of disease. Some parents will even dub a child Hodoh, The Ugly, to persuade demons he is unattractive prey. . . . 'In Kelantan five or seven bananas are dubbed with persons' names: they are laid before the infant and he is given the name allotted to the particular banana he grabs first.' The Perak Malays have a series of conventional names for their children in order of seniority. A Malay will often drop his own name and be called 'Father of Awang', or whatever is the name of his first-born. Like the Brahmin, he refers to his wife never by name but as 'the person in my house', or, when she is older, as 'the mother of Awang' or 'so and so'. The idea underlying this custom appears to be that a demon cannot attack one whose name he does not know.

If the child is a raja, young mothers of good family suckle him or her in turn, their own children thus becoming foster brothers or sisters of the infant. The royal mother may confirm this by suckling the infant of the foster mother.

Muslim custom prescribes the seventh day for the formal naming of the child, the shaving of its hair, and the sacrifice of two goats for a boy and of one for a girl. This is followed in Malaya. One lock of hair is left on a boy's head as on the head of Brahmin children and of Egyptian Muslims, but it is a custom of primitive Malays also to leave a lock un-shorn as a refuge for the child's soul. Sometimes this tonsure ceremony may be deferred for girls until marriage. At one such deferred ceremony the headman and the girl's nearest relatives clipped the ends of seven locks with seven strokes of the scissors, an exact though unconscious imitation of Brahmin ritual. When the head of a royal baby is shaved, the wives of the great Perak chiefs each snip a few hairs in turn according to their rank. Notable, too, is the opening of the child's mouth by a ceremony performed also in Arabia and Egypt, but perhaps reaching the Malay from India. A gold ring is dipped in a mixture of betel-juice and sugared and salted water, and an elder utters a Muslim adjuration of which the original occurs in the Rig-Veda: 'In the name of Allah, the Merciful, the Compassionate! May he lengthen your life! May he teach you to speak fittingly in the court of kings! May he give to your words the attractiveness of betel, the sweetness of sugar and the savour of salt!' The gold ring is tied to the child's wrist. And any religious teacher of piety and learning is invited to spit upon the child's head or into his mouth to endow him with intelligence and ability to learn to read the Kuran.

The exact likeness of a boy to his father, that is, the possession by two hosts of one soul, disquiets a Malay; one of the boy's ears must be pierced, otherwise father or son may die. The resemblance of a girl to her father or of boy or girl to a mother is of no moment.

When the forty-four days of purification are complete, the midwife throws away the platform on which the young mother has been warmed and the ashes of the fire that has burnt by her side. And now, just as the Brahmin and Siamese royalty take a child out to see the sun, so the Malay introduces his child to 'Mother Earth and Father Water'. The midwife carries the baby to the top of the stair or house-ladder, recites incantations and marks a cross on the soles of the infant's feet with lime. She descends and puts the child's feet first on iron (the blade of a wood-knife or the head of a hoe) then into a tray containing gold and silver (usually a ring of each metal) and lastly on the earth. That is the custom in Upper Perak, but details vary in different places. In Kelantan a raja's child has to be taken down from the house by three steps, no more, no fewer. He is carried through a line of women holding lighted candles to a spot where seven gold plates are placed. The first plate contains herbs, the second unhusked rice, the third husked rice, the fourth rice-paste, the fifth yellow turmeric rice, the sixth earth from a grave, and the seventh sand from the sea. Into each of these plates the child's feet are pressed before they are allowed to tread the earth. Then the baby raja is carried up a seven-tiered stand and bathed. After the lustration, the stand is thrown, with the spirits attaching to it, into the sea.

Next the Malay infant is carried down to the river. A candle is lit and stuck on a boulder or bamboo staging. Mother and midwife descend into the stream. The mother bathes the hair of the midwife and then the midwife performs the same service for the mother. An offering is made to the water-spirits: an egg, a quid of betel, seven long and seven square rice-packets. The usual three kinds of rice and rice-paste are sprinkled over the surface of the river. The child is passed through the smoke of incense. Then a live fowl is placed in the water and the child made to tread on it, so that he may have power over all domestic animals. Next a sprouting coconut seedling is set afloat and the infant's feet are placed on it, so that he may have power over all food plants. Lastly a jungle sapling, usually a rattan creeper, roots and all, is put in the stream and the setting of the little feet upon it gives the child dominion over the forest. A palm-spathe bucket and a banana-flower are turned adrift. If the baby is male, a boy catches a fish with a casting-net; if the baby is female, a girl should throw the net. Finally a man casts the net over a group of the midwife, mother and infant, and a crowd of tiny children representing fish.

After this ritual introduction to earth and water, the infant is laid for the first time in a swinging cot fashioned of black clothes hung from a rafter. Into the bunt of the cot are put a cat, a curry-stone, and an iron blade to mislead and terrify evil spirits. Then the midwife lifts the baby into his new home. Pious old ladies croon lullabies. Muslim prayers are recited. There is a feast on curry and rice.

In the water for a baby's ablutions are steeped the same collection of strong-souled substances that are put beside the garnered grain of the rice fields. If the attacks of spirits have made him sickly, the leaves of a plant called the Genie's Tongue (*Hedyotis congesta*) may be infused in his bath. If the baby cries continually, he may be 'smoked over a fire made of the nest of a weaver-bird, the skin of a bottle-gourd, and a piece of wood that has been struck by lightning'.

Great care is taken of the placenta, the child's 'younger brother' (or sister), which is kept for a while and then buried, generally under a tree. If the new-born child is royal, boys of good family, five to seven years old, are chosen for this function. Their leader envelopes his head in a black cloth and on it carries the placenta in a new earthen pot to a place selected for the burial. Sometimes the boys ride there on elephants. In Perak the coconut seedling (*nyiur gajah*) used at the infant's introduction to water is planted to mark the site. Head and face still enveloped, the leader of the band returns to the royal cot, greets its occupant with the Hindu *Om* and hails him as brother of himself and his followers.

(b) Adolescence

Magical precautions accompany circumcision, teeth-filing and the boring of girls' ears. Even the observances at handing a child over to the care of a religious teacher and at the conclusion of his studies, Muslim as they now are, may be a survival of Hindu ritual and some more primitive initiation ceremony.

Some form of circumcision is practised at puberty among the heathen tribes of the Malay Archipelago, in the Philippines and in Polynesia. 'It is only one of the many mutilations of the body that are performed by primitive mankind in order to counteract the evil influences arising at puberty,' influences comparable to those of a menstruous woman or mother in child-bed. To-day it is regarded by Malays as a Muslim obligation. A boy undergoes it at any lucky and convenient age between six and twenty. Often it is done immediately after the celebrations at the conclusion of his religious studies. At the Perak court, amid great festivities, a young raja is clothed like a bridegroom in State dress. The State Magician pours oil upon water in which the acid juice of limes has been mixed. From the pools of oil that float in the shape of moon and stars, he tells if the moment is propitious for the ceremony, and if the boy will later marry a girl of his own class. Then he rubs the mixture on the forehead, hands and feet of the boy and of his companions who will undergo the operation at the same time. Feasting may last for days. Royal candidates are borne in procession—in Perak on painted elephants or men's shoulders, in Negri Sembilan in a royal processional car, in Patani on a huge coloured model of Visnu's Garuda. In Patani, too, sham weapons of wood are carried in front of them. In Kelantan a torchlight procession goes seven times round the house of the chief where the function is to be held; wooden or palm-leaf walls are removed and the procession perambulates the house without descending to the ground. In Perak sometimes the boy is seated on a bridal dais, has a dance with lighted candles performed before him and his fingers stained with henna. There, too, a raja lies full length on the floor and is covered with a silk cloth, his body sprinkled with saffron rice and cooling rice-paste, and his

mouth stuffed with a lump of glutinous rice and three
grains of parched rice. A hen is passed all along his body,
then placed on his chest and encouraged to peck up any of
the grains of rice that may be sticking to his lips. If she is
slow to peck, it will be long before the boy marries. Two
coconuts and a small bag of rice are rolled over him from
head to heel. Just before the operation the boy is escorted
to river or well, where the same offerings are thrown to the
spirits of the water as when he was first introduced to that
element. Custom demands that members of his family,
male and female, bathe along with the sufferer. In one folk-
tale when the princely hero was about to undergo the rite,
his two sisters in the palace soaked fingers and toes in a jar
of water. The one long lock of hair that has been a symbol
of childhood is shorn by his mother or nurse or the man
who later is to circumcise him. During this tonsure a mock
fight is started with bundles of rice, till the water resounds
as if buffaloes were fighting in it, a custom recalling the
mock combat to clear rice-fields of demons. A princeling
of the Perak house may be seated on the topmost tier of a
pavilion built on the river bank and have charmed water
poured over him through a white cloth. Then he is led
down into the stream and the first to be dragged after him
will be his father, the ruler, who is drenched with sand and
water at the hands of the great chiefs and courtiers. The
final ceremony takes place indoors. The boy is seated on
the stem of a banana or on a sack of rice, and at the Perak
court a swordsman stands beside him so that if aught goes
wrong 'the plug for the wound and the dressing may be
taken from the operator's corpse'. At the same court
throughout the various stages of the ritual, at the taking of
the omens, at the procession to the river, and at the operation, the royal drums are beaten and the royal flutes and
trumpets blown. The sufferer's food consists of dry fish or
buffalo meat and his plate is lined with a parched banana-leaf,

the dryness of diet and leaf having a homoeopathic effect on his unhealed wound. Till the wound is well, he may not wear a cap. For months before the operation he is warned not to eat tough meat. These and other rules are dictated by mimetic magic. If he was born with a caul, a piece of it preserved from his birth is often given him to eat in a banana.

An analogous but merely nominal ceremony of a very private nature is observed for girls also, either in infancy or early youth, a midwife being the surgeon.

Puberty brought also for both sexes the practice of filing and blackening the teeth in order to substitute for sharp white fangs, 'like those of a dog', an even row of teeth, black 'like the wings of a beetle'. One of the incantations recited is for personal charm and pre-eminence and shows signs of travestying the Sufi's 'perfect man'. In a folk-tale called 'Awang Sulong' the operation was done with one rasp of the file a day and one a night for nine days and nights, and the beauty of the glossy black stumps of the hero made folk ask

> *Whose the cock that struts so bravely,*
> *His lips a shore beset with bridges,*
> *Bridges of black shining palm-spikes,*
> *Teeth as stems so sharp and knitted,*
> *Mouth a boatful of red nutmegs,*
> *Ebon teeth like bracelet circle?*

The object of this practice was, it has been surmised, to sacrifice a part to save the whole of what was particularly full of soul-substance or, perhaps, it was due to an idea that not coition but breath is the direct cause of conception, when mutilation of the teeth, like circumcision, is a device to neutralize the dangerous energies of puberty. The stumps were blackened, it has been surmised, to conceal from the spirits the partial nature of the sacrifice. Blackening of the teeth has died out, but filing is still practised, even after marriage, to beautify the teeth and prevent their decay.

Girls' ears are bored either in early childhood or at puberty, with the usual magic ritual to worst evil spirits. At the Perak court in the eighteenth century two nights were devoted to henna-staining before the ears of a ruler's daughter were pierced, and on the second night she was escorted on an elephant seven times round the palace. The needle employed is threaded with cotton of many colours, having at the ends turmeric cut in the shape of a floweret: two of these flowerets adorn the thread left in each ear. Just as the boring begins, those present throw money into a silver bowl, perhaps to drown any cry or murmur. After this, large ear-studs used to be worn during a girl's maiden days but are now donned only at her wedding to be discarded formally on the consummation of the marriage. At the Perak court the ceremony is concluded with a feast and prayers in honour of the Prophet and of the parents and ancestors of the ruler.

(c) Betrothal and Marriage

There is little or no magic about a Malay betrothal. It is a contract to be ratified before headman or elder, and to be published abroad by the despatch to the girl's relatives of two elaborate betel boxes, one of them containing one or two rings wrapped in betel-leaf. If the youth is guilty of breach of promise, the girl's people keep the ring or rings: if the girl is guilty, her parents return them with cash their equal in value. In parts of Perak the betel boxes (whose shape recalls the little ship used in Majapahit) are replaced by trays, one of which is adorned with a paper tree; and, when the bearers arrive, yellow rice is strewn. The boxes or trays are proffered only if negotiations for the marriage are successful. Nowadays girls are seldom married before they are fourteen or fifteen, or boys before the age of seventeen: often both are older. Like the Hindu, the Malay considers a hairy person unlucky. The Brahmin student may not feed 'the husband of a younger sister married before the elder, the husband of an elder sister whose younger sister was married first, a younger brother married before an elder, an elder brother married after a younger', and in Malaya, also, the request for a younger sister's hand before her elder sisters are wedded is universally disliked. In the figurative language of Malay betrothal verses the suitor comes, like the Esth wooer, 'in search of a lost calf', just as among the Finns he wants to buy a bird, and among the Sardinians to ask for a white dove or a white calf. The suitor accepted, his mother is invited within, where she slips the ring (or two rings) on the finger of her future daughter-in-law. Songs and feasting conclude these preliminaries.

Seven days later the suitor and his friends resort to the girl's house and stay singing and feasting for two days and two nights. Before leaving, the suitor does obeisance to his future mother-in-law. When harvest time comes, he and his friends are invited to help, and the rice that will be eaten at the marriage is trodden out to the accompaniment of songs bandied between men and women, the two parties of groom and bride. But in Negri Sembilan a youth is ashamed to meet either of the parents of his future bride, even accidentally on the road.

Favourite times for weddings are after the harvest or after the season of rice planting, not only because those are days of leisure but probably because at the latter season the child in the womb and the grain in mother earth are likely to develop simultaneously. The festivities may occupy two or four or five days if the contracting parties are humble peasants, seven or forty days or even months if they are rajas. Astrological tables are consulted to determine a lucky time to begin them.

On the first day the magician takes steps to protect the groom, and a matron to protect the bride from all jealous spirits. In Upper Perak this preludes a most elaborate marriage ritual. The magician ties a ring on a white thread round the bridegroom's neck; lights a candle on cup or tray; burns incense and invokes all spirits and the sacred dead to be kind. He scatters saffron rice, sprinkles the groom with the usual cooling rice-paste and dresses his hair. A matron does the same service for the bride. If her shorn fringe lies close to the forehead, it is a sign that she is a virgin; if it sticks up, then 'the flower has been sipped by a bee'. (At the Perak court the midwife first waxed and clipped seven long hairs: if the stumps moved or the tips fell towards the girl, she had been deflowered.) On either side of the house-door a red and a white flag are stuck. The magician descends the house-ladder. sprinkles the earth with yellow rice and rice-paste, and offers betel to the spirits of the soil. The bride is bathed in her house. The groom is conducted down to the river. A white flag with a candle fixed on its shaft is planted on the bank. Near by, two large candles are put on the ground. Incense is burnt in three bamboo cressets, to which are tied three candles, three quids of betel, and three native cigarettes. On a vertical frame is fastened a palm-blossom. Again rice is scattered with appeals to all the spirits of earth and water. The palm-blossom is broken open that the dew in its heart may be mixed with limes and rice-powder for bathing the bridegroom. During the lustration he stands in the river facing downstream and has water thrown into his mouth. The white thread is broken from his neck and he is dressed in a raja's garb. A scion of the Perak royal house will be lent the armlets and jewellery used at the installation of the ruler; then, mounted on elephants with painted foreheads, he proceeds with religious chanting and song to the house of the bride. An umbrella is held over the bride-groom's head and his attendant fans him. On arrival the groom steps down into a tray of water, in which are a stone, a ring, a razor, and a dollar. He is sprinkled with saffron rice and seated on a dais. For three nights, singing and firing crackers, youths encircle a 'henna tree' in a bowl containing henna and stuck with lighted candles. The experts seize and dance with it in turn until one of them carries it up the house-ladder, where girls receive the 'tree' and take up the dance. To extinguish the candles during inversions and gyrations is the sign of a boor. On this first night both bride and groom are stained with henna in private, and the formal marriage before an authority from the mosque may now take place. All the fingers of the girl are stained; three of the man's, counting from the little fingers. On the second day a Perak princess of the highest rank used to be taken in procession with flags, umbrellas and music, seven times round the palace. On that night the fingers and palms and toes and the sides of the feet of the married pair are stained with henna in public. Dramatic shows, dancing girls, and feasting entertain the guests. The rice for the *confarreatio* on the morrow is brought out, piled in tiers on an octagonal platter, topped with a tinsel tree and stuck with dyed eggs on skewers. The couple sit in state, and guests pay homage to the bride now and to the husband at the sitting in state on the following day.

On the third day there are chants in praise of Allah and the Prophet. A buffalo is slaughtered. The girl's relatives escorted by music present decorated rice, coconuts and fire-wood to the relatives of the groom. The bridegroom is escorted thrice each way round a circular dome-shaped frame containing incense, that is, in a passage between its mat sides and a white cloth held up by those present. After-wards he is placed inside the frame and censed for the space it takes a dancer with a branched candlestick to circle the structure three times. Next the bride is brought out to undergo the same ordeal. The bride goes to her room. A duenna guards the door. There is a mock combat between the sexes. The magician demands entrance for the bridegroom, and is admitted after presenting a betel-box that contains a ring and some cash. His instructor lifts the groom's left hand and puts it on the bride's head. The couple have to feed one another with betel. Then three, five or seven old people paint the palms of the couple's hands with henna and sprnkle them with rice. After that they are stripped of their finery, led three times in each direction round an inverted rice-mortar and seated upon this symbol of sex and fecundity. They are lifted thrice before they are declared duly seated. The magician pours fresh coconut oil into a bowl of water, and after throwing five grains of rice on the oil, drops the wax of a lighted candle on to the mixture. The pair are bathed with this compound, together with water from blossoms of the areca and coconut palms. Coconut fronds are waved seven times above their heads. Bathing accomplished, varicoloured string is dropped round and over the heads of the pair three times while they step forward, and then under their feet and upwards three times while they step back. After that performance the string is lowered to their chests and severed over the right rib of the groom and the left of the bride. If the front piece is longer, the wife will obey her husband; if the back piece is longer, the 'rudder will be at the bows', that is, the wife will rule the roost; if the two pieces are equal, both will hold their own.

The next ceremony obtains everywhere. Husband and wife don royal costume (or nowadays the man may wear Arab dress)—this, it has been surmised, 'shows both the tabu character of bride and bridegroom, and also an attempt at disguising them by fictitious change of identity'.

Perhaps it was the same notion that originally impelled the Mantra and the matriachal people of Negri Sembilan to give a new name or title to a bridegroom on his marriage. The couple now sit in state on a dais, the husband on the right of the wife. Sumptuary custom fixes the number and colour of mats and pillows allowed, according to the rank of the contracting parties. There is an exercise in Swedish drill, where the performer has to sink slowly down into a squatting posture, straighten his knees and stand erect. This exercise the embarrassed pair have virtually to fulfil, until after three efforts they are seated simultaneously as custom ordains. The pyramid of rice topped with a tinsel tree stands before them just as before a king of Siam at his coronation were set two artificial trees as 'emblems of future blessings'. The pyramid is broken up and the pair have to feed one another three times with clots of the rice held in their fingers. After that they must remain motionless, like a ruler at his installation, while those present do obeisance to the 'royalty for a day'. Guests throw money into a bowl. Muslim prayers may be read. At last the principals are allowed to retire. Each guest is given a dyed egg out of the rice pyramid to take home.

On the following days there is more lustration and feasting.

Throughout all these ceremonies bride and groom remain silent and no glances are exchanged between their downcast eyes.

If a husband is disappointed in the virtue of his bride, he may advertise his disillusionment by appearing without head-dress or creese and he can claim back half the dowry. But a marriage is not consummated for three nights or more. So it is not usually till the seventh day that, with little fingers interlaced or both holding one handkerchief, the couple are bathed again with all the precautions described for the bathing on the third day. The seven fronds waved over them are dropped for bride and groom to step to and fro across them three times, after which the fronds are cast out of the house taking ill-luck. A censer is passed about the pair and a cord of vari-coloured thread is tied around their necks joining them. At this ceremony the guests, also, are drenched with water from buckets and bamboo squirts. (At royal weddings, before they are bathed, the pair are carried in procession three or seven times round a storeyed pavilion built for the lustration.) After being bathed, both don finery once more and sit in state.

Sometimes on the night before this final lustration the groom's friends tear him from the dangerous fascination of his wife's arms by lighting a smoking fire to bring him to the door, whereupon he is carried off to his parents' home and only escorted back next day for the bathing ceremony.

Everywhere it is usual for the husband to live in his bride's home for some while after the marriage. Among the matrilineal Minangkabau colonists of Negri Sembilan he lives in it permanently.

The ritual of Upper Perak on the border of the Siamese Malay States contains some novel details. The circumambulation of a structure containing incense and the lustration of the couple before the day when the big sitting in state takes place have not yet been recorded from the south.

The order of marriage ceremonies varies according to locality and the means of the parties. Sometimes the Muslim service is performed just before the sitting in state. Sometimes the mimic combat for the bride's person, a custom practised in ancient India and in Europe, takes place on arrival at her house and is repeated before the bridal dais.

The throwing of rice over the head of a bridegroom is commonly observed by Indo-Germanic peoples. *Confarreatio*, or eating together, is a world-wide usage. In many parts of India and Europe and in Muslim Morocco the bridegroom is treated as a king on his wedding day.

The Code of Manu lays down that among the elements of a Brahmin's wedding are the leading of the bride three times round the sacred fire, each time with seven steps, and the binding together of the wedded pair by a cord passed round their necks. Again, 'On the second or third day of Brahmin marriage ceremonies,' says Thurston, 'sacrifices are performed in the morning and evening and the *nalagu* ceremony. The couple are seated on two planks covered with mats and cloth, amidst a large number of women assembled within the *pandal*. In front of them betel leaves, areca nuts, fruit, flowers and turmeric paste are placed on a tray. The women sing songs they have learnt from childhood. Taking a little of the turmeric paste rendered red by the addition of lime, the bride makes marks by drawing lines on her feet. The ceremony closes with the waving of water coloured red with turmeric and lime, and the distribution of betel leaves and areca nuts. The waving is done by two women who sing appropriate songs.' In many parts of India bridegroom and bride are seated on mortar or pestle or grinding stone.

A Malay raja may remain away and send his creese or his handkerchief to represent him when he marries a wife of humble birth. It is so that a Hindu girl is married to a prince or a god. An obsolete raja custom was to send a creese to parents who were reluctant to give their daughter in marriage, with a message that the suitor was ready with dower and presents doubled: if they remained obdurate, the creese had to be returned with double the dower offered. Another method, with a Sanskrit name, was for the suitor to force entry into the house, secure the girl, and drawing his creese defy resistance. If the ruse succeeded, the man had to give twice the usual dower, present two garments instead of the customary one and pay double the ordinary fines for trespass. These two ways of wooing are of Indian origin.

The painting of the couple with henna to fend off evil

influences, the first night in private, the second in public; the dance with the henna bowl and lighted candles—these ceremonies occur at Muslim marriages even as far away as in Morocco. Islam has added items to the ritual of Malay marriage but has failed to banish others incompatible with its tenets. The sitting in state and the lustration of the pair before mixed audiences of men and women offend the strict, but retain so strong a hold on the Malay imagination that a bigoted chief, whom I knew, reluctantly observed them, but in a loft under the roof, where guests could not scale!

When the bride is a widow, particularly a childless widow, the marriage rites are greatly curtailed and often confined merely to the short legal service before the Kathi.

(d) Death

At a rock-shelter near Sungai Siput in Perak there have been discovered skeletons lying on their backs, the bones of bodies moved for final interment after the flesh had perished, and skeletons completely flexed. In the Malay archipelago all three types of burial are common; and in New Zealand, for example, the bodies of chiefs are extended and those of others flexed. But in modern Malaya the oldest type of burial for civilized or Deutero-Malays is the tree-burial of the shaman (p. 21) of which a variant is exposure on a platform. Many of the graves of bygone sultans of Perak are raised platforms, so that one wonders if they are a survival in culture of the tree-platform, though graves waist-high were built by Hindus for holy men.

Apart from the rare (and now obsolete) tree-burial of the shaman, the civilized Malay has long observed the rites of Muslim burial. Before that the Hindu had taught him to cremate. How he treated his dead before the Hindu period can only be inferred from his surviving superstitions and

from the customs of Malaya's aborigines. Of these aborigines, the Negrito (who anthropologically is the oldest)
would appear to have practised tree-burial and believed in
a sky-world, and branches of all Malaya's aborigines have
reserved tree-burial for the honoured shaman. The Indonesian Sakai, who have ceased to be nomads, either abandon
the house where there is a corpse and leave it there or else
they bury their dead. The proto-Malay buries his dead and
has constructed a remarkable type of grave.

In the Pyramid texts there is often mention of a ladder
up which dead Egyptian kings could climb to the sky. And
close to a Besisi grave is built and furnished a temporary
hut with inclined stick-ladders to enable the soul of the
deceased to climb into it. Beside the grave of a proto-Malay
chief who died in Johore in 1879 there were similar small
upright sticks to enable his spirit to climb out. Sticks five
feet tall with seven upward and seven downward notches
are also recorded. Another account says that there are seven
downward notches almost wholly underground to prevent
the ascent of the deceased's spirit and six upward notches
above ground to ensure that the spirits of the living shall
climb upward and not join the dead. Dayaks are said to fix
a stick-ladder 'upside down' in the path near a cemetery to
check the wanderings of any departed spirit.

The Johore 'chief was buried three feet deep under a
mound about three feet high; round it was a ditch where
the dead might paddle his canoe. That such a ditch was
nothing strange is shown by a Kelantan prescription for
obtaining a shaman's powers. Sitting one at the head and
one at the foot of the grave of a murdered man the would-
be shaman and a companion must burn incense and make
believe to use paddles shaped from the midrib of a yellow
coconut palm, calling the while upon the murdered man
to grant magical powers. The landscape will come to look
like a sea and an aged man (probably Luqman al-Hakim,

the father of Arabian magic) will appear and duly supplicated grant the request. The Johore ditch and the Kelantan
myth both recall a form of burial common in the Malay
world, in which canoe-coffins are employed for the dead
emigrant to return to his original home or voyage to an
island afterworld. It is interesting evidence of a seafaring
race.

A hut, such as is built near a Besisi grave, may have been
meant once for the temporary sojourn of the soul but
appears now to be for the grave-ghost, which by Malaya's
aborigines is supposed to haunt a grave for seven days. For
seven days the proto-Malay will sound no drum near a
grave for fear of recalling the dead. For seven days he will
kindle a fire to keep the hovering soul warm and he will
place food on the grave to provision the departed for his
journey to the after-world. The belongings of the dead are
also put on the grave. Sometimes his blowpipe will be
broken because it is tabu to use the weapons of a dead man
or perhaps because in the spirit world the broken looks
whole and the whole looks broken.

Very little of all this ritual has been retained by the Muslim Malay. But still for seven days after a death lights must
be lit and the bed of the deceased prepared, and near the
house of the dead no rice may be ground and no music or
dancing be performed. Among pagan tribes of Borneo a
drum is beaten to announce a person's death to his friends
in the afterworld, the number of strokes indicating his rank,
and similarly at the obsequies of a Malay sultan the state
drums are beaten and the state trumpets blown. Then for
seven or even twenty or forty days they are hushed. After
the death of one of his chiefs a sultan may order that for
five or seven days the state band shall be mute. It is forgotten that originally silence was kept not to guide the
ghost of the dead back to his temporal home, and silence
now is only a mark of respect.

The body of an important person is escorted under umbrellas to the place of ablution, where men or women, according to the sex of the deceased, support it on their extended legs. A chief's corpse will be washed by all the local mosque officials and Hajis. His insignia will be exhibited round his body, which is laid upon a dais of the type prepared for all formal functions. As the corpse is being shrouded, forty Hajis offer prayers. For it is believed that among every forty who offer the prayers there will be a saint whose request will be heard.

A chief's bier is a huge platform, which it may take a hundred men to lift. A bier may be of several storeys. The bier of the commoner chief of Jelebu, for example, is of five storeys; the bier of a raja is of seven. At the Jelebu rites a lad chosen from a privileged tribe scatters coin from the topmost bier; nine maidens of the same tribe are seated on the litter, eight keeping the corpse in position with their extended hands and the ninth holding a young plantain tree as a symbol that 'the broken grows again' and the chieftainship of Jelebu never dies. At the funeral of royalty sixteen girls used to support the body. Outside the Minangkabau colonies of Negri Sembilan the tree symbol is not found in the Peninsula. Children are made to pass under a parent's bier before it is carried to the grave, not only as a token of respect but to prevent them from pining for the deceased.

In many places strips are torn from the pall and worn by relatives of the dead on arm or wrist to keep them from undue longing for the departed. This is the practice in Negri Sembilan and at the obsequies of a sultan of Perak. The *Malay Annals* record an instance where the pall of a tributary prince was despatched to his suzerain with the news of his demise. Generally Malay mourners wear workaday shabby clothes, and at a royal funeral it was expected that all a ruler's subjects should go without headdress and with dishevelled hair. For three days after the death of the chief of Jelebu no man may wear any head-dress except a white cap, Hajis must discard their turbans and women their veils. When the most famous ruler of Perak in the eighteenth century came to the throne, for seven days the royal drums and trumpets were silent in honour of his predecessor, and on the eighth the new raja's head-dress was brought on an elephant by the Bendahara, the chief who rules temporarily during the interregnum between ruler and ruler; Sultan Iskandar 'Inayat Shah donned it, and only then did his courtiers cover their heads. (The new Sultan dismissed from office and broiled in the sun many persons who had failed to arrive for the obsequies!) Sometimes for forty days after a ruler's death no head-dress is worn. But in place of the baring of the head, Malays have introduced now a very popular fashion of wearing a white band round the hat. And black clothes are frequently worn.

It is considered unlucky to attend the funeral of one who has died a bad death, or of one whose corpse turns a dark livid hue, and mourners hurry away. Like the Chams, the Malays still have funeral feasts on the third, seventh, fortieth and hundredth day after a death. There are some who (like the Brahmin student) will not partake of a funeral feast, especially on the third and seventh days after the death, because jinns have often been seen pouring into rice and curry water that has run off the corpse at the final ablution. Take a strip of the shroud, a chip of the coffin-plank, and a broad leaf to hide behind, and one can see them, some with children on their backs, like human beings, catching the water in jars!

Temporary wooden posts are often planted at a grave, until permanent stones can be got. If the deceased has left a child frantic with grief, then every night for three or seven successive nights a vessel of water is tied to the temporary tombstone by a shred of the shroud, and every morning the child is bathed in the water. In Perak, on the hundredth day the temporary posts are cleansed with limes and rice-paste, thrown into the river and have water sprinkled over them thrice to drive away evil influences.

Sometimes over the tomb of a saint or ruler there is fixed a mosquito-net or a light frame and canopy or a palm-thatched roof, under which lamps and candles are lit.

Expensive and well-built houses are killing the Indonesian custom of abandoning the hut where a death has occurred. But in the past a Malay ruler would seldom occupy the palace of his predecessor. And even now a wooden house is sometimes taken to pieces and re-erected on a fresh site.

APPENDICES

APPENDIX I
The Malay Original of Passages Quoted

Page 27

IN the *Atharva-Veda* (ed. M. Blomfield, Sacred Books of the East, vol. XLII, p. 358, Oxford, 1897) is printed a love-charm, of which the Malay translation is as follows:

Bismi' llahi 'r-Rahmani 'r-Rahim.
Bakar bakar pasir tanah!
Aku bakar mata hati jantong (si-anu) itu.
Bakar-ku panah Sang Ranjuna,
Aku bakarkan di-gunong, gunong runtoh,
Aku bakarkan di-batu, batu belah.
Aku bakarkan di-mata hati jantong hawa nafsu (si-anu).
Kena hanchor luloh panas segala tuboh-nya
Gila berahi kapada aku,
Tidak boleh senang diam;
Saperti pasir ini terbakar.
Benchi-lah (si-anu) kapada ibu bapa,
Kapada saudara sahabat handai-nya;
Jika dia tidor, menjadi jaga;
Jika dia jaga, membangun berjalan
Datang kapada aku
Menyerahkan diri-nya:
Hilang 'akal, hilang malu.
Berkat (si-anu) kena bisa panah Sang Rajuna,
Berkat do'a, 'La ilaha illa' llah, Muhammad Rasulu 'llah.'

To make this spell effective the Malay fried sand from the girl's footprints night and day without oil.

There is an English translation of the charm in my book *The Malays* (London, 1958).

Page 29
>Mari-lah enchē'! Mari-lah tuan!
>Uraikan rambut-kau yang panjang lampai.

Page 29
>Hai nēnēk! Terima-lah persembahan ini!
>Pinta-lah, rakit kita selamat melaluï jeram panjang.
>   Jangan-lah apa-apa 'aradl gendala di-tengah jalan.
>   Buka saperti mayang mengurai!
>   Buka saperti ular mengorak!

Page 29
>Asal embun menjadi ayēr,
>Asal ayēr menjadi buēh,
>Asal buēh menjadi batu,
>Asal batu menjadi bijēh.

Page 30
>Bukan aku jijak atas bumi;
>Aku pijak atas batu kepala sakalian yang menyawa.

Page 30
>Sinar mencherang akan muka-ku;
>Bintang timor akan mata-ku;
>Gajah jantan akan badan-ku;
>Harimau buas akan sandar-ku;
>Buaya ganas kedudokan-ku.

Pages 30–1
>Om si-Kumari! Mahadēwi om!
>Aku anak si-rimau ganas!

APPENDIX I

Chuchu baginda 'Ali!
Gemuroh akan suara-ku,
Halilintar akan mata-ku,
Kilat akan senjata-ku
Bergentar bumi, bergentar-lah aku,
Bergerak bumi, bergerak-lah aku.

Page 31

'Kau turtu kata-ku!
Jikalau 'kau ta' turut kata-ku,
Mati di-bunoh Seri Rama;
Jikalau 'kau turut kata-ku,
Di-hidupi Maharishi.

Page 31

Perkataan ini bukan perkataan aku,
Perkataan Sang Narada,
Perkataan Sang Samba.

Pages 40–2

Bismi 'llahi 'r-Rahmani 'r-Rahimi!
Hai dato' petala bumi, jin tanah!
Berhala besi! . . .
Menyiah engkau, jin dan shaitan!
Kuderat Allah hendak lalu.
Ah si-jeranjang! si-jeranjung!
Tundok-lah engkau!
Anak harimau jantan lalu—
Hai jin dan shaitan!
Jembalang, jembali!
Jangan engkau ka-mari menempoh larangan firman
    Allah taala!
Jikalau engkau menempoh larangan firman Allah
    taala,
Durhaka-lah engkau kapada dzat wajib al-ujud.

Aku taku asal engkau jadi;

Tanah Bukit Si-Guntang Mahamēru asal mula engkau
jadi. . . .

**Yang diam di-awang-awang si-lēla si-menjamun nama
engkau;**

Yang diam di-langit si-juak nama engkau;

Yang diam di-kayu ara si-tinjau nama engkau;

Yang diam di-ayēr si-kerakah nama engkau;

Yang diam di-jalan si-jeranjang nama engkau;

Umanat Allah kapada aku

Rasul Allah akan junjongan-ku!

Kiraman Katibin akan senjata-ku!

Jibra'il, Mika'il, Israfil, 'Azra'il akan saudara-ku!

Tujoh lapis kota besi tempat ku-diam.

Ya Malik . . . turun berperang memeliharakan diri-ku!

Menurunkan do'a si-panchar matahari penundokan
Raja Malin (?Malaun),

Sedang Raja Malin lagi tundok khidmat kapada aku,

Kunun ra'ayat tantera-nya jin dan shaitan jembalang
jembali tundok kapada aku.

Ah! si-k . . . ! si-kunchai-kunchai! si-tongkat-tongkat!

Terkunchi-lah gigi engkau yang dengki khianat kapada aku;

Terkunchi hati jantong limpa engkau yang berniat
jahat kapada aku!

Aku tahu asal engkau jadi,

Saktimuna asal engkau jadi.

Ah! engkau bersusah hati! engkau sesak!

Engkau memandang, mata engkau pechah!

Engkau menyerodok, punggong engkau burok!

Nēnēk yang diam di-telok rantau tanah ayēr sa-rantau
ulu sa-rantau hilir,

Yang diam di-bukit belukar rimba batas gaung gun-
tong

Sa-kampong ulu, mata ayēr, kayu besar, batu besar!

Bawa-lah ra'ayat tantera engkau,
Bawa-lah anak pinak engkau
Kapada si-rendang yang besar
Ujong tanah di-bawah kaki bukit Kaf.
Jangan-lah aku di-rosak di-binasakan!
Di-timpa daulat firman Allah taala engkau!
Karna aku serta Allah dan serta Muhammad Rasul
    Allah
Serta anbia' Allah dan aulia Allah,
Serta malaikat yang empat-puloh empat,
Jibra'il, Mika'il, Israfil, 'Azra'il!
Aku serta Kuran tiga-puloh juz.
Nabi Noh yang memegang bumi,
Nabi Elias yang memegang kayu,
Nabi Khidzr yang memegang batu,
Luqman al-Hakim yang memegang besi,
Nabi Sulaiman yang memegang segala yang bernyawa!
Aku memohonkan bumi, ayer, kayu, batu,
Tempat membuat negeri kampong laman rumah
    tangga.
Hai segala yang bernyawa!
Jangan-lah kami di-rosak di-binasakan!
Jikalau di-rosak di-binasakan kami,
Di-timpa daulat firman Allah taala engkau
Dan berkat mu'jizah Muhammad Rasul Allah dan
    anbia' Allah,
Dan keramat segala aulia Allah,
Dan keramat segala malaikat empat-puloh empat,
Jibra'il, Mika'il, Israfil, 'Azra'il.
Ah nēnēk kerakah tua, nēnēk kebayan bandan peli-
    harakan kami!
Jangan di-rosak di-binasakan kami!
Jikalan di-rosak di-binasakan kami,
Durhaka-lah engkau kapada Allah!

Pages 40–2—continued

Jikalau mata engkau yang ēlah dengki,
Mata engkau di-pechahkan Allah!
Jikalau tangan kaki engkau yang dengki khianat,
Tangan kaki engkau di-patahkan Allah;
Jikalau hati jantong limpa engkau yang berniat dengki khianat,
Hati jantong limpa engkau di-hanchorkan Muhammad,
Di-hanchorkan Baginda Rasul Allah.

Pages 42–3

Hai jin kafir! jin Islam!
Kita orang sa-asal, sama hamba Allah.
Tetapi engkau jadi daripada chahaya api nuraka,
Aku jadi daripada chahaya nur Muhammad;
Engkau anak jin saktimuna.
Aku anak chuchu Nabi Allah Adam;
Engkau ummat Nabi Sulaiman,
Aku ummat Nabi Muhammad.
Engkau pun hamba Allah,
Aku pun hamba Allah.
Jangan-lah engkau menyakiti segala ummat Muhammad!
Jikalau engkau sakiti dan engkau binasakan segala ummat Muhammad,
Durhaka-lah engkau kapada Allah
Dan kapada Rasul Allah
Dan kapada segala anbia' Allah dan aulia Allah
Dan kapada malaikat yang empat-puloh empat,
Jibra'il, Mika'il, Israfil, 'Azra'il.
Ah jin dan shaitan, jembalang jembali!
Menyiah engkau dari sini
Kapada si-rendang yang besar
Ujong tanah di-bawah kaki Bukit Kaf.

Jikalau engkau tiada menyiah ka-sana,
Durhaka-lah engkau kapada dzat wajib al-ujud
Bait al-Mukaddis tanah terjali.
Hitam mērah tanah ku-letak di-gulang-gulang;
Hantu tanah! jembalang tanah! jangan engkau me-
ngulang-ulang.

Page 47

Tepong tawar! tepong jati!
Dapat emas berkati-kəti.
Aku menepong tawar beras padi;
Sudah berisi, maka menjadi.

Page 47

A's-salam alaikum
Hai Nabi Allah Sulaiman, raja sakalian bumi!
A's-salam alaikum
Hai jin tanah! jembalang bumi!
A's-salam alaikum
Hai bapa-ku langit!
A's-salam alaikum
Hai ibu-ku bumi!
A's-salam alaikum
Hai bapa kawal, ibu kawal!
Aku 'nak kirim anak-ku, anak Maharaja Chahaya
pada ibu-nya;
**Aku suroh belayar ka-laut hitam, ka-laut ijau, ka-laut
biru dan ka-laut ungu!**
Aku kirimkan enam bulan;
Ketujoh ku-sambut naik;
Bukan aku menurunkan benēh,
Aku menurunkan padi.

Page 48

Hai Langkēsa! Langkēsi!

135

Diri berempat, berlima dengan kami!
Jangan di-rosak di-binasakan anak kami!
Jikalau di-rosak, berubah setia dengan kami!
Di-makan besi kawi-lah engkau!
Di-timpa daulat Pagar Ruyong!
Di-timpa Kuran tiga-puloh juz-lah engkau!
Kabulkan Allah!

Page 49

Hai jembalang akhir! jembalang awal!
Jembalang sa-ratus sembilan-puloh!
Jembalang kaki! jembalang aku!
Jembalang bakul! jembalang batang!
Jembalang bukit! jembalang gunong!
Jembalang padang! jembalang aku!
Engkau undor simpang sa-belah!
Kalau engkau ta' undor, ku-sumpah engkau.

Page 50

Hai semangat, anak-ku, Maharaja Chahaya!
Aku kirim pada ibu awal enam bulan, ketujoh ku-
  sambut naik;
Sampai perjanjian ku-sambut naik;
Ku-suroh belayar ka-laut hitam, ka-laut hijau, ka-laut
  biru, ka-laut ungu;
Ka-benua Rum, ka-benua Keling, ka-benua China dan
  ka-benua Siam.
Aku 'nak sambut ka-atas anjong istana,
Ka-atas tilam perhiasan permadani.
Aku suroh chari indong pengasoh pengiring.
Chari ra'ayat bala,
Temenggong, Bendahara, Kuchang, Laksamana;
Menchari kuda gajah, itek angsa, kerbau kambing dan
  biri-biri
Berhimpun timbun gegak gempita.

APPENDIX I

Mari ka-sini! Chukup lengkap!
Aku 'nak panggil 'mu mari!
Hai semangat, anak-ku Maharaja Chahaya!
Mari-lah enchēk! Mari tajok! Mari sunting! Mari
    malai!
Abu 'nak sambut 'mu naik ka-anjong istana,
Ka-atas tilam perhiasan permadani.
Hai semangat anak-ku, Maharaja Chahaya!
Mari-lah 'chēk! 'Nak sambut.
Jangan-lah kasēhkan indong pengasoh-mu!
Hai sabun putēh! sabun hitam! sabun hijau! sabun
    biru! sabun ungu! sisir sa-belah!
Chahaya jin shaitan sisir sa-belah!
Chahaya yang sa-benar chahaya anak-ku.

Pages 51–2

Hai Dang Pok! Dang Malini!
Bertompok dayang di-sini.
Dang Pok! Dang Malini!
Tetap dayang di-sini!
Bergerak langit tujoh lapis,
Bergerak anak-ku Maharaja Chahaya!
Ta' bergerak bumi tujoh lapis,
Ta' bergerak anak-ku Maharaja Chahaya!
Tegoh saperti batu keras,
Saperti besi tetap-lah,
Dari dunia datang ka-akhirat,
Tetap sa-kali dengan tuboh badan ayah dan bonda-
    nya.
Bercherai Allah dengan Muhammad,
Bercherai 'mu dengan aku;
Ta' bercherai Allah dengan Muhammad,
Ta' bercherai 'mu dengan aku.

137

Page 73

Ashahadu Allah ilaha-illa' llah
Wa ashahadu inna Muhammad Rasul Allah!
Ya saudara-ku Jibra'il, Mika'il, Israfil, 'Azra'il!
Engkau berempat! Berlima dengan aku!
Aku dudok di-kerusi Allah.
Aku bersandar di-tiang 'arash.
Aku bertongkatkan tiang Ka'abah.

Pages 73–4

Puchik-ku tersandar di-tiang 'arash.
Allah mengulor, Muhammad menyambut.

Page 74

Dudok aku di-bawah 'arash Allah,
Payong-ku Muhammad serta-ku,
Jibra'il di-kanan-ku,
Mika'il di-kiri-ku,
Sidang malaikat mengiringkan aku,
Khalifat Allah . . .
Berkat aku serta Allah
Berdiri 'ku serta Muhammad,
Bermara Allah, maka bermara aku,
Bermara Muhammad, maka aku bermara-lah!
Ular tedong akan chawat-ku,
Gajah meta akan kendaraan-ku,
Kilat pantas akan tentang-ku,
Harimau buas akan bayang-ku,
Berkat aku memakai do'a si-Awang Lebēh;
Dudok pun aku lebēh,
Berdiri pun aku lebēh,
Berjalan pun aku lebēh,
Berkata-kata pun aku lebēh,
Berkat do'a si-Awang Lebēh,
Aku-lah di-lebēhkan Allah di-dalam dunia.

APPENDIX I

Page 76

Bismi 'llahi 'r-Rahmani 'r-Rahimi!
Hai sahabat-ku penghulu Iblis!
Hai segala hantu shaitan
Yang suka mengachau orang!
Aku minta-minta-lah kapada dato'-dato'
Minta pergi-lah
Masok ka-dalam perut (si-anu) itu,
Gorēngkan mata hati jantong-nya,
Saperti pasir ini tergorēng;
Gila berahi 'kan aku.
Bawa datang
Suroh menyembah menyerahkan diri-nya
Berkat buat nasi dan nap-uap
Buboh dekat dapor ini,
Atau enchēk-enchēk ingat baik-baik.

Pages 77–9

Barang siapa hendak mengamalkan 'ilmu kota tauhid ini, di-bacha fatihah dahulu, dan di-hadiahkan kapada yang empunya dia. Maka di-mulai pada malam Juma'at pula, di-bacha-nya empat kali sa-malam serta di-nadzarkan hati kita bersunggoh-sunggoh kita mengesakan kapada Allah serta di-shuhudkan masok ka-dalam fuad kita, sa-hingga penoh maujud di-dalam diri kita pun, di-'itikadkan-lah, 'Aku ghaib di-dalam dzat mutlak dan itlak', maka fana-lah diri mutlak dan itlak jua.

Allahumma salli 'ala sayiddinā Muhammadin wa 'ala 'āli Muhammadin. Hawwat-tu 'alā nafsi dan taulan-ku dan segala anak-ku dan segala isi rumah-ku dan harta-ku dan barang yang di-milēk oleh tangan-ku dengan tujoh kota daripada Allah taala; atap-nya itu, 'Lā 'ilāha illā 'llahu' dan dinding-nya, 'Muhammadun rasulu' llah,' dan anak kunchi-nya kudrat Allah, tiada terbuka sa-lama-lama-nya melainkan dengan idzin Allah. Muhammad itu saperti manusia, tetapi tiada saperti manusia, ia-itu saperti yakut antara batu.

Shahadan ada pun murad daripada kota itu telah kita ketahuï asal kita itu daripada 'adam, melainkan kembali kapada 'adam pula kita. Ada pun yang ada nyata-nya itu hanya ujud Allah jua samata-mata-nya.

Bahawa ada pun akan ujud Allah itu sa-kali-kali tiada bercherai dengan dzat-nya yang mutlak itu bagi dzat-nya, maka ia-itu-lah yang melakukan barang kehendak-nya, saperti firman-nya, 'Fa'alun li-mā yuridi', erti-nya berlaku barang kehendak-nya atas diri-nya jua, tiada berkehendak kapada yang lain-nya daripada-nya itu, sa-sunggoh-nya pun kapada 'adam jua. Tammat.

Shahadan ada pun murad daripada diri itu ruh nama-nya, suatu sifat daripada 'ilmu Allah taala, tiada bercherai dengan dzat-nya, dan ia-lah jadi suatu hakikat-nya, maka di-namaï insan. Ada pun ruh itu mufassal lagi muqayyad. Bahawa sa-nya ruh itu berkehendak sentiasa kapada Tuhan-nya. Tammat.

Shahadan ada pun murad daripada rumah itu jasad nama-nya. Ada pun jasad itu tempat (?) pergetaan ruh itu, karna itu-lah sa-benar-benar-nya tempat kenyataan hak Allah taala, saperti sabda Nabi salla'l-lahu 'alaihi wa's-salam, 'Man 'arafa nafsahu, fakad 'arafa rabbahu', erti-nya, 'Barang siapa mengenal diri-nya, maka bahawa sa-nya mengenal Tuhan-nya.' Ada pun rumah itu di-jadi sendiri-nya; sunggoh pun lagi akan fana, melainkan empunya rumah-nya hak yang kekal dengan dzat-nya yang mutlak itu.

Shahadan ada pun murad daripada harta kita ia-itu saperti hati dan jantong dan paru-paru dan hempedu dan barang yang di-jadikan Allah taala, samata-mata-nya saperti firman-nya, 'Wa mā tashā' ūna 'lla'an yashā'a 'llahu rabb'ul-'ālamīn', erti-nya 'Tiada kuasa sa-orang jua melainkan dengan kuasa Allah kapada sakalian 'alam ini daripada dzahir dan batin-nya.' Tammat.

Shahadan ada pun murad daripada milēk pada kita itu pancha indera yang sa-puloh itu : pertama, dzahir; kedua, batin. Ada pun yang dzahir itu lima perkara : penglihatan mata, penengaran telinga, perasaan lidah, penchium dengan hidong, penjabat dengan tangan. Ada pun pancha indera yang batin itu lima perkara pula : sirr, 'itikad, chita, rasa dan ·l· wa hum baina ākhar!' Tammat.

Shahadan ada pun murad daripada tujoh kota itu, karna Allah taala menjadikan kita ini tujoh sifat; maka di-sempurnakan insan itu tujoh sifat—sifat hayat, 'ilmu, kudrat, iradat, sama', basar, kalam. Dan wajib sujud kapada Allah itu tujoh anggota: pertama-nya dahi, kedua-nya tapak tangan, ketiga-nya lutut, keempat-nya kaki dengan perut-nya jari.

Shahadan ada pun murad daripada kunchi itu, sebab sangat-sangat yakin kita dan tauhid kita pada menyerahkan diri kita kapada Allah taala, saperti firman-nya, 'Wa tasimū bi-habli 'llāhi yami 'an wa lā tafarrakū' erti-nya, 'Berpegang kamu dengan tali Allah yang tiada putus', lagi tiada terlindong barang sa-kehendak-nya itu daripada ma'rifat-nya, saperti kata Nabi salla'l-lahu 'alaihi wa's-salam, 'Lā tataharraku dzarratun illā bi-'idzin 'llahi', erti-nya, 'Tidak bergerak barang suatu jua pun melainkan dengan idzin Allah'. Karna tiada dapat di-pandang itu dengan memutuskan, dan tiada putus melainkan dengan kehendak Allah samata-mata, maka tiada dapat lain-nya. Tammat.

Shahadan ada pun murad daripada anak kunchi itu Muhammad Rasulu' llah, karna Allah itu sangat-lah ter-bunyi, tiada siapa mengetahuī akan dia melainkan pada diri-nya. Sebab itu-lah Allah taala memelihara kebesaran-nya itu, maka Hak Allah taala pun tajalli kapada ruh Nabi kita Muhammad 'maka ruh itu-lah Allah taala menjadikan sakalian 'alam ini, maka dzahir-lah sakalian sifat 'ilmu-nya yang batin itu. Sebab itu-lah di-katakan anak kunchi karna membuka perbendaharaan yang terbunyi, saperti firman-nya, 'Kun-tu kanzan mukhafian' erti-nya, 'Ada aku harta yang terbunyi.' Tammat.

Shahadan ada pun murad daripada pelihara Allah, saperti firman, 'Wa Huwa ma'akum aynamā kuntum', erti-nya, 'Allah taala serta kamu, barang di-mana ada kamu', saperti firman-nya, 'Allah terlebēh hampir daripada urat lēhēr.'

Shahadan ada pun murad daripada atap itu kuasa Allah atas barang yang di-kehendaki-nya pada menudong daripada sa-orang hamba dengan rahmat, maka jadi-lah ter-kunchi daripada sakalian seteru-nya dan bala-nya daripada dunia ka-akhirat; maka tiada-lah terbuka kapada sakalian jin dan manusia melainkan dengan idzin Allah taala. Tammat.

APPENDIX II

(a) Father Sky and Mother Earth

The Mantra, a proto-Malay tribe, claim to be descended from Mertang, the first magician, who was the child of two persons called Drop of Water and Clod of Earth. In the Moluccas the earth is a female deity, who in the west monsoon is impregnated by Lord Sun-Heaven. The Torajas in Celebes believed in two supreme powers, the Man and the Maiden, that is, the sun and the earth. The Dayaks of Borneo hold that the sun and the earth created the world. 'Father Sky and Mother Earth', occur also in a mixture of Sanskrit and the vernacular in Bali—*Bapa (a)kaca: babu pret(h)iwi*. In Malay they are addressed not only by the shaman but by the master of the shadow-play, before the drama of Rama and Sita is enacted; but then the player is an incarnation of Visnu, of whom Rama was an avatar.

For the Malay as for the Babylonian and the Brahmin Sky is in the background, a mere counterpart of Earth which in India was deified under many names, including Prethiwi (or Pertéwi) and Bhumi, both terms borrowed by the Malay.

In China the worship of heaven was the concern of the Emperor, whose court conducted a sacrifice on the longest night of the year. Formerly in Malaya, the king as an incarnation of Hindu godhead was also the intermediary with heaven, though the older shaman might continue to invoke Father Sky. In Perak the court offered annually a nocturnal sacrifice to state genies who are nearly all of them sky-gods, though contaminated for several centuries with the deities of Indian romance. The adoption of the Hindu pantheon and divine king has led to the apparently erroneous notion that except in the Timor group sun-worship has not been practised in Indonesia. In Timor, as in China and Malaya, the sun-god was worshipped once a year and was regarded as too exalted for mundane affairs and ordinary worship.

For a prospective bride or bridegroom to eat food out of a stewpan on the eve of marriage is sure to bring showers to mar their wedding-day, presumably because their action involves tilting the pan that symbolizes the sky. Rice-spoons are closely associated with cooking-pots. To kill a storm the Malay fisherman will tie a rice-spoon across his mast in the direction of the wind and command it to die before this pointing. While in other regions blood is spilt as a sympathetic charm to induce the falling of rain, in Pahang, again under Sakai influence, an animal is sacrificed so that its blood dropping on the earth may cause the torrent of rain to cease, or, if an animal cannot be procured, the villagers will cut their own hands or feet. That is, if no one knows what broken tabu has caused the downpour. If one knows, it suffices to count seven and cut the hair of the person at fault, whereupon the storm stops. This last custom recalls the Malay sailor's prayer to the wind to let down her long flowing tresses and may be intended to stay 'the rustle of rain' by imitative insulation from its source. Australian aborigines use human hair for rain-making.

Rice-planters often soak a cat to procure rain, the reluctant quadruped being regarded apparently as a pleasing sacrifice. To kill a snake, whose skin looks always moist, or to dress up a frog in a cradle will cause disastrous floods, rain and these animals being so closely associated that insult to them invites vengeance from their protector. In parts of Pahang where Sakai influence is strong, to tease any undomesticated animal, to celebrate a mock marriage between dog and cat or between coconut monkey and crab-eating macaque, to push a weaver-bird's nest with one's punt-pole and make it spin or to play with a wild bee's nest are all methods of causing terrific storms and landslides. It is to be noted that the tormentors must always mock their victims, and that when the flood comes, it is only these mockers who cannot escape, every spot where their feet tread becoming soft.

(b) The Nigget

There is a tradition that to acquire a nigget a Sakai hag will dance stark naked and dandle a child's corpse into the similitude of life before biting off its tongue. A Cham prophetess must resort on the night of her initiation to a ant-heap in the moonlit forest, sever a cock from head to tail and dance naked, uttering incantations that will restore the fowl to life. For many of the ceremonies of black magic nudity is prescribed, either because abnormal ritual goes with abnormal acts or because the celebrant would exhibit utter submission to the spirit invoked or because indecency can shock a spirit into compliance. Islam has banished nudity from Malay magic. But probably a ritual older than Islam first forbade the Malay fisherman at his stakes to insult the gods of the sea by bathing naked. Wilfully to expose the person in an indecent manner is the grossest form in which one Malay can insult another.

The seizing of that organ of eloquence, the tongue, was also a feature of a forest rite among the Tlingits of Alaska. There when a shaman died, his novice retired to the forest where the dead man's spirit sent him usually a land-otter whose tongue he wrenched out, exclaiming, 'May I be skilful to charm and to dance.'

(c) Siva as the Spectre Huntsman

The Spectre Huntsman is known to the Malays by the various names of Siva, such as Raja of land-folk, Raja of

Ghosts and Gaffer Long Claws, the tiger. Siva was the Rudra of Vedic times and Rudra has the same characteristics that distinguish Wodan (or Odin) namely those of a storm-god followed by hosts of spirits, a leader of lost souls, identified both in Malay and Teutonic legend with the Spectre Huntsman or Indo-Germanic god of the tempest. Brahmans bare themselves to the waist before a superior and less than a century ago waiting-maids at the Perak court so bared themselves to serve a ruler in whose ancestors had been incarnate Hindu gods. So the shaman at a *séance* (where Siva is always invoked) is naked from the waist up and no one wearing a coat may approach a patient stricken by the Spectre Huntsman, If a man crossed by him suffer from fever and vomiting, the spell muttered by the Perak medicine-man must reveal the knowledge that the Spectre Huntsman has no navel, a clear indication of godhead. In the Mahabharata Siva is described as 'exceedingly tall' and in Pahang when not engaged in the chase the Spectre Huntsman is called the Tall Spectre, who like Siva is identified with the father of all jinns.

Again in the Mahabharata Siva is said to be of the form of all the points of the compass and one Malay invocation speaks of 'the four children of Siva who dwell at the corners of the world'.

(d) *Spirit possession of the inanimate.*

Possession is not only of animate things. At the installation of a Sultan of Perak the guardian genies of the state may inhabit the state sword and make it press upon the ruler's shoulder. In the regalia ritual they are invited to descend on posies, perhaps flowers stuck behind the ear of the magician, as the yellow *chempaka* blossom is still stuck behind the ear of a ruler at his installation. The convulsive shaking of the shaman's grass switch may indicate that they enter there. Sweet jasmine attracts them. A Perak chief, who knew how to make from the shroud and coffin of a murdered man powder rendering spirits visible, enabled a friend at a *séance* to see two women with streaming hair descend through the roof and alight on a flower-vase, the artificial garden prepared for their advent.

According to one account the spirits invoked at a *séance* enter the flame of candles and cause them to flicker. If the flame flickers towards the shaman, he can undertake to cure his patient; if it flickers away from him, he cannot. A similar use of tapers is made to choose a spot suitable for building a house or an elephant corral. If the burning wick inclines towards the diviner, the omen is good; if away from him, bad. If it bends to the right or the left, a site in that direction should be chosen. If it becomes twisted or droops or burns with a double flame like the twin stones over a grave, the site is unlucky. If it burns upright, the omen is excellent. A Kelantan chief will fashion two candles of identical size with wicks of seven or nine threads, name one for himself and one for his foe and, calling upon Allah to declare the future, infer victory for him whose candle burns longer. Even if the candle at a *séance* is regarded merely as a means of divination, yet the Malay mind supposes it to be animated by a spirit and its answer to be dictated by this lodger.

In one Malay dance an old woman, who must have an 'impressionable soul', makes a sheaf of palm-blossom sway in time to the music, jump about and dash itself to the ground. In another a fish-trap dressed as a female scarecrow rocks and dances at the bidding of the magician. The puppets for Malay shadow-plays are 'all considered to be more or less animated'.

(e) *The Malay Spell*

The spell may require to be supplemented by contagious and by homoeopathic or mimetic magic. Sand from the footprint of the woman loved, earth from the graves of a man and woman, the hair-like filaments of bamboo, black pepper: these are often steamed in a pot while a love-charm is being recited. Another method is to 'take a lime, pierce it with the midrib of a fallen coconut palm, leaving one finger's length sticking out on either side whereby to hang the lime. Hang it up with thread of seven colours, leaving the thread also hanging loose an inch below the lime. Take seven sharpened midribs and stick them into the lime, leaving two fingers' length projecting. The sticking of the midrib into the lime is to symbolize piercing the heart and liver and life and soul and gall of the beloved. Put jasmine on the end of the midrib skewers. Do this first on Monday night, for three nights, and then on Friday night. Imagine you pierce the girl's heart as you pierce the lime. Recite the accompanying charm three or seven times, swinging the lime each time you recite the words and fumigating it with incense. Do this five times a day and five times a night in a private place where no one shall enter or sleep.' A woman recites a charm for beauty over the water in which she bathes or over the coconut oil with which she anoints her hair.

Even in Vedic times, however, often no ritual was required and the mere recital of the verbal charm sufficed. An Indian would mutter in the presence of a hostile witness: 'I take away the speech in thy mouth, I take away the speech in thy heart. Wherever thy speech is I take it away. What I say is true. Fall down inferior to me.' So, too, the Malay to-day without any ritual recites: 'O God! let the world be blind, the universe deaf, the earth stretched out dumb; closed and locked be the desire of my enemy'; or he whispers,

> *Om! king of genies!*
> *The rock-splitting lightning is my voice!*
> *Michael is with me!*

In virtue of my use of this charm
To make heavy and lock,
I lock the hearts of all my adversaries,
I make dumb their tongues,
I lock their mouths,
I tie their hands,
I fetter their feet.
Not till rock moves
Shall their hearts be moved;
Not till earth my mother moves
Shall their hearts be moved.

In Malay as in Hindu charms the curse plays a weighty part:

I would wed the image in the pupil of my mistress'
*   eye*
With the image in the pupil of my own!
If thou lookest not upon me,
May thy eyeballs burst!

Or again:

Genies of supernatural power!
Your home is at the navel of the sea,
By the tree on the broken rock!
Enter not the line drawn by my teacher!
Else will I curse ye with the words,
'There is no God but Allah and Muhammad is His
*   Prophet.'*
Om! I neutralize all evil,
O Solomon! In the name of God.

For the Malay, too, as for the Hindu the origin of a thing or spirit gives magical control over them. In the Atharva-Veda the mention of the names of the father and mother of a plant, for example, is a typical part of a magic formula. Incense is hailed by the Malay magician as a product of the brain of Muhammad, 'its smoke the breath of his spiritual life'.

Rice paste:

> *It came down from Allah's presence,*
> *From a drop of dew descended!*
> *From the water whence eternal*
> *Life comes—that it's source of being.*

(f) *The Bridge of the Dead*

Among the negritos of the Andamans and Malaya, the Indonesian aborigines of Malaya, the Bataks, Dayaks, Torajas, Bugis and many other Indonesian peoples of the Malay archipelago and as far afield as Melanesia there has survived the idea of a bridge leading to an afterworld.

There are local variations of the myth. The negritos of the Andamans and of Kelantan talk of the bridge being invisible, some of Malaya's negritos describe it as a green switch-back over a sea, most of Malaya's negritos as well as the Milanos think it is a log-bridge and the Milanos say that the souls of the just cross it and reach paradise but the souls of the unjust fail and tumble into an icy purgatory. All the aborigines of Malaya declare that the just can cross it but the wicked fall into a boiling lake. In Nias the pagans talk of a sword-bridge over a river. And the idea has often been supposed erroneously to have come from the Muhammadan belief in a bridge finer than a hair and sharper than a sword over which the good pass, while the wicked topple from it into hell. But the notion is too widespread and is found among primitive people too remote to have got it from such a late source or even from the Zoroastrian belief in the bridge Chinvat, which Islam borrowed from the Avesta. The idea occurs in China, in Scandinavia, among Mongols, Tartars and Turks, and among Jews and Greeks.

There is one feature that suggests the idea was imported into Indonesia, Polynesia and Melanesia from outside. The negritos of Kelantan say that the heaven across the bridge is reserved for wise men like a shaman who is therefore given tree-burial to help him fly over the head of the giant that guards the passage. Throughout Indonesia rank and lavishness over the funeral feast and sacrificial offerings are required if the dead are to win to paradise. In Melanesia and Polynesia it is rank or tribal marks or funeral feasts that qualify for the sky-world. These qualifications point to the introduction of the idea by immigrants who claimed to belong to a higher or ruling race.

A widely spread belief is that the bridge is the rainbow. In the Eddas there is a rainbow bridge to Valhala. The myth is found in Polynesia. And the Indonesian Senoi of Malaya believes in a rainbow snake that stretches to the region of hell.

The tree-trunk bridge of the Kelantan negrito is guarded by a giant with one nostril, two eyeless sockets, curly-haired, long-nailed and tusked. The Besisi of Malaya make the guardian a dog; the Milanos say a two-headed dog flings ashes at souls as they try to cross. And this notion of a formidable watchman to prevent the evil from crossing the bridge is also far spread, occurring also in the Eddas. Perhaps it arose from a belief in a river-spirit demanding sacrifice and feasts of appeasement for the trespass of the bridge-builder.

Only a shaman can recross the celestial bridge back to the world of the living, the shaman of the proto-Malay Benua, the Cham shaman, the Tungu shaman who in his trance rides to heaven on the rainbow. On the skin of a shaman's drum the Altai-Tartars depict heaven, a rainbow and the deer on which the shaman makes his journey. In Celebes among the East Torajās a shaman rides on the rainbow which is also a boat.

The Benua and the Cham shaman ascends to heaven in the strains of a musical instrument, returning with a divine gift of flower or plant to cure a patient's illness. The drums of the Malay shaman and of the Malay ruler are sacred and can harm the profane. In Bougainville Island it is the drum at the funeral-feast that denotes the opening of the gate into the spirit land. The most famous drums in south-east Asia are the bronze drums of a civilization termed Dongsonian after the site of a *câche* in Annam. Like Dayak funeral paintings, they depict soul-boats in which shamans escort the dead to the sky after-world. These Indonesians from Dong-son got their art and designs and presumably beliefs from Europe. It has been suggested it was brought before 720 B.C. by the Tokharians, one wave of whom helped to destroy the Chou capital in 771 B.C.

M. Räsanen, Regenbogen–Himmelsbruke, Studia Orientalia XIV, I., Helsinki, 1947; *Pagan Races of the Malay Penninsular*, Skeat & Blagden, 2, pp. 203, 208, 300; *Negritos of Malaya*, I. H. N. Evans, 1937, pp. 256–7, 263–4; *Life after death in Oceania and the Malay Archipelago*, R. Moss, *v.* Index *sub* Bridge, 1925; *On the Aboriginal Inhabitants of the Andamanese Islands*, 1932, p. 94; *Dictionary of Religion and Ethics*, ed, J. Hastings *sub* Bridge, Shaimanism, and State of the Dead; *The Perilous Bridge of Welfare*, Dona Louisa Commaraswamy, Harvard Journal Asiatic Studies, 8 (2), 1944, pp. 196–213; *Das Tocharer—Problem und die Pontische Wanderung*, R. Heine-Geldern, Saeculum, Vol. II, 1951, pp. 225–55; *Prehistory and Religion in South-East Asia*, H. G. Quaritch Wales, London, 1957.

(g) *A Relic of Saktism*

In *Malay Poisons and Charm Cures* by Dr. J. G. Gimlette (London, 1929, pp. 79–94 and 274–280), and in *Danses magiques de Kelantan*, by Jeanne Cuisinier (*Travaux et mémoires de l'Institut d'Ethnologie XXII*, Paris, 1936, ch. 8), there are descriptions of a propitiary ceremony to cleanse that Malay state (*pūjā negeri*) by *séance*, dancing, and sacrifice, conducted by a male or female shaman termed for the occasion 'princess' (*putrī*). Who was this 'princess'?

Folklore speaks of a *putrī* Sadong adopted by a queen of Kelantan 600 years ago and also of a *putrī* Sakdom.[1]

The invocations employed, though covered with a Muslim veneer, point to the survival of Tantric ritual. Every *Tantra* should begin with an account of the creation, go on to worship the Hindu gods, and conclude with the modes of union between God and man. So the Malay ritual, as recorded by Dr. Gimlette, begins with the (now Muslim) story of the creation, and follows it with invocations to Father Sky and Mother Earth, the Ganas, Arjuna, nature spirits, genies, the Spectre Huntsman (or Siva as Rudra), and Kala or Siva the destroyer. The concluding incantation (recorded only from a curative *séance*) conceals its Tantric origin under Sufi imagery. In the Bhagavad-Gītā it is said of the Eternal Spirit 'everywhere are its hands and feet'; and the Kelantan shaman adjures malicious spirits that the organs of his patient are the habitations of the four Archangels and the first four Caliphs and that on his feet move Allah and His Prophet.

The Tantric order of the incantations guides one to the identification of 'the princess', who can be none other than the *élan vital* personified in the feminine principle or Sakti of Siva. Without that principle Siva (and crops) would die, and so his Sakti can properly play her part in ritual designed to end an epidemic or promote a good harvest. '*Tantras* describe the worship of a woman, a young girl, sometimes a child (*kumārī pūjā*) who is treated exactly like an idol. She is bathed and bedecked, placed inside a diagram and turned into a divinity by the laying on of hands. Then she is honoured by flowers, incense, lights, and food. In her is the spirit of the supreme Sakti. Afterwards the devotee from time to time passes the night with her' (*L'Inde classique*, L. Renou and J. Filliozat, Paris, 1947, p.

---

[1] Final -*i* in Kelantan becomes -*ing* and final -*ing* becomes -*im*; the consonant in a last syllable is unstressed and vague.

596). 'When the deities summoned at a Tantric *sādhana* are 'girls' or 'princesses' or 'ascetic goddesses' (*yoginī*), we have to deal with the worst features of paganism' (L. de la Vallée Poussin in Hastings' *Encyclopaedia of Religion and Ethics*, sub. Tantrism). The group of men and women that celebrated these orgies survives apparently in the Kelantan shamans male and female who join the chief performer in *séance* and dancing.

It is possible that there is a vestige of the time when the Kelantan 'princess' was a woman in the name of 'bridegroom' (*pengantin*) borne by the chief performer's assistant fiddler and chanter. And the transition from the 'princess' being represented by a woman to her inhabiting even a male shaman would not be difficult in a cult where every worshipper sought to be identified with the Sakti.

In Kelantan, as in Assam (*The Saktas*, by E. A. Payne, London, 1933, p. 87), Saktism was a religion confined to Rajas. To-day there is no survival of it in any other Peninsular State, though there are historical traces of Tantrism in Perak, Pahang, and Trengganu, and in the Malay archipelago. A Mahāyāna bronze of Avalokītesvara from Bidor in Perak, bearing among other symbols a noose, is evidence that about the ninth century A.D. the Pala dynasty of Bengal had introduced there a blend of Mahāyāna Buddhism, Saiva rites and Tantric orgies. At a Kedah site (Archaeological Researches, H. G. Quaritch Wales, JRAS, Malayan Branch, xviii, pt. 1, 1940, p. 56 and pl. 60) of the ninth or tenth century A.D. was found a gold miniature model of the broad spatulate dagger associated in Java with Siva in his Tantric form of a demon Bhairava and in Sumatra with the Minangkabau regalia, which includes such a blade inlaid in gold with the figures of a fourteenth-century ruler, Adityavarman and his consort arrayed as Bhairava and Bhairavi (De Rijkssieraden van Pagar Roejoeng. Dr. F. D. K. Bosch, Oudheidkundig Verslag, Batavia, 1930):

an inscription of 1347 records their performance of a dance for the fertility of the crops. In an old spell from a Perak MS. (Maxwell Malay MS. 106; Royal Asiatic Society) the consort of the Forest Lord, i.e. Siva, is called Tiarabeh Gandi, apparently a corruption of Bhairavi (or Bhagavati = Tara or Sakti) Chandi, 'The Awful, the Fierce'. In India human sacrifice to Siva's Sakti as Kali, goddess of death, was common, and in Malaya, too, it occurred. In 1349 Wang Ta-Yüan records of the people of Trengganu, a state adjoining Kelantan: 'they carve wood into (images) of gods and sacrifice to them with the blood of men, whom they put to death for the purpose, mixed with wine. Whenever there is a drought or plague, they pray to them. . . . Furthermore, whenever a man or his wife is very ill, they have their fortunes told' (Rockhill's *Relations and Trade of China with the Eastern Archipelago*, T'oung Pao, vol. xvi, 1915, p. 119). That is a good description of a shaman's *séance* and of Tantric sacrifice. And, correctly or not, it is repeated for Pahang in the Hsi yang fan kuo chih of 1434 and by Fei Hsin in 1436 (ibid., pp. 74 and 121).

So the Kelantan 'play of the princess' would appear to blend (a) appeal to spirits through the shaman's familiar, appeal pagan and primitive, (b) the embodiment in a shaman priest or priestess of Siva's Sakti, and apparently the *chakra-pūjā*, (c) tantric dancing for fertility, and (d) the sacrifice of buffaloes instead of the former male human victim.

In the photographs taken by Dr. Cuisinier the Kelantan shaman looks an Indian, like the Brahmans who still officiate at the courts of Bangkok and Pnompenh, though he was not only locally born but a Muslim. His office was hereditary.

In a 'Note on Saktism in Java' Dr. W. F. Stutterheim suggested that the ancestral or tribal mother of the Indonesian became the *ādisakti*, the spirit representing matter from which everything in earth and heaven sprung, the supreme self-existent power of nature, the universal mother, the first cause. 'She was the Prajñaparamita of the Buddhists, the Laksmī of the Vaisnavas and the Dewi of the Saivas.' (*Acta Orientālia*, vol. xvii.)

(h) *Kingship and Enthronement*

There are two rulers in Malaya who claim descent from a Bichitram (?=Vicitram), reputed kinsman of the Srī Mahārājas of Sri Vijaya, the Buddhist empire (fl. A.D. 750–1350) that extended over Sumatra and Northern Malaya and for a while Java. The name Bichitram is whispered into the ear of every Perak Sultan at his enthronement as that of the ancestor of the Perak (and old Malacca) dynasty. And Bichitram, according to the *Sejarah Melayu*, was brother of the first king of Palembang (=Sri Vijaya) and Singapore, and was himself ancestor of the Minangkabau line, from which the Yang di-pertuan of Negri Sembilan claims descent.

Whatever their genealogy, it is the enthronement of the two Malay rulers claiming this descent from Palembang or Sri Vijaya that interests the ethnographer, being as everywhere marked by many survivals in culture.

To understand the awe Malays have had for their rulers one has to explore the origin of their divine right. In his latest avatar, a Yang di-pertuan, He-who-is-made-master, is the Shadow of Allah on earth, whose blood is held to be white as in the veins of Muslim saints. But formerly it was as an incarnation or receptacle of a Hindu divinity or a Boddhisatva that he was credited with white blood, and the rulers of Perak and Negri Sembilan are still installed with Brahminical and Buddhist ceremony. Moreover, under the Muslim Caliph and the Hindu-Buddhist ruler, there remain traces of the shaman from Yunnan and affinities with the emperors of China and Japan. The custom in

Japan and formerly in Malaya of vacating the palace of a dead predecessor and starting a new capital, the custom of giving dead kings posthumous titles, the couch-throne found in Japan's oldest enthronement ritual and in parts of Indonesia, the reverence for regalia without which no Japanese or Malay can become a ruler, all these would appear to belong to a very early layer of civilization.

The Malay King as Shaman

Both Malay ruler and Malay shaman were masters of the mannikin soul of things (p. 10 *supra*). And if as seems certain ideas derive from great centres of civilization, then conception of the power of Malay kings and magicians will have come in prehistoric times to the Malays, as to China of the Chou period, from Babylonia or some other centre in the Middle East, to be carried from Yunnan down to the archipelago; a conception to be developed centuries later into the idea of a Malay king being a Hindu god, and to conclude in the Malay's ready acceptance of Islamic pantheism with the famous cry of Abu Sa'id that 'there is nothing inside this coat but Allah'.

As a Hindu god the Malay king was lord of the realm by virtue of possessing a miniature Mount Meru. But as Confucius reminds us, even five centuries before Christ there was 'an earth-mound at the borders of a Chinese town or village, interpreted as symbolizing the whole soil of the territory in which it stood. It was often associated with a sacred tree or grove and with *a block or pillar of wood* which served as a resting place for spirits'. Under the old wooden palace of Negri Sembilan hangs by a rope a carved truncated pillar (or oblong block) of wood, not reaching the ground and tabu for all but royalty. As we shall see, a palace or a temple came in time to symbolize the mound mentioned by Confucius.

The office of shaman, like that of ruler, is often hereditary among Malays, and both possess as insignia drums and tambourines baleful to those that touch them, even though the ruler's vengeful instruments have become part of a Muslim's *naubat* band. It is tempting to surmise that it is with the grass aspergillum of the shaman a Sultan of Perak sprinkles rice-paste on newly installed chiefs, but the brush of medicinal leaves used by the King of Siam before his coronation is prepared by Brahmins. However, as late as 1874, Perak folk saw nothing strange in their Sultan, 'Abdu'llah, sitting at a *séance* on the shaman's mat and becoming possessed by the genies of the State, who prophesied the death of the British Resident. Just as Japan had a spiritual head in the Mikado and a secular in the Shogun, so however it came by him, during the last two centuries at least Perak had in addition to its secular ruler a Sultan Muda holding the office of State Shaman, whose duty it was annually to revive the regalia by proffering them food and drink and on occasion to sacrifice to the guardian spirits of the country, brought within the fold of Muslim orthodoxy by inclusion under djinns who are all subservient to Allah.

While the Sultans of Malay port kingdoms waxed rich on tolls and dues, it is perhaps significant that like the shaman (and the Khassi chief) a Sultan of Minangkabau had no source of income beyond the produce of the royal demesne and voluntary contributions for ceremonial functions. But, though the Malay shaman frequently uses a tabu vocabulary, there appear to be no words reserved for himself and his actions, as there now are for rulers. It is notable, however, that in the old Indonesian tongue, Sundanese, the words *siram* 'bathe', *gering* 'dry = sick', *ulu* 'head', *běrangkat* 'be carried = travel', *titah* 'order', *mangkat* 'borne away, dead' are not, as in Malaya, reserved for royalty and tabu for others. Moreover the words 'be carried' for the royal mode of progression, 'borne away' as a euphemism for death, and 'dry' for 'sick' embody Hindu ideas that a king must never set foot on earth and that his subjects must never allude to him as liable to mortal ills.

The Malay King Incarnate as a Hindu God

Along with those Indonesian words tabu in Malaya for all but royalty have been joined the Sanskrit words: *murka* 'angry', *kurnia* 'gift', *anugrah* 'give'. For to graft the Hindu conception of a divine king on to the Indonesian master of magic was in many respects easy. A man might be born a shaman or he might be made one by magic rites, just as a Hindu king, though hereditary, acquired divinity by the performance of the magic ritual of enthronement, which under a Muslim veneer is still for Malays a Hindu and Buddhist ceremony.

(1) As in Vedic times, as formerly in Burma and still in Siam and Cambodia, the first rite is lustration. In Perak the Sultan sits on a banana-stem, while water is poured down a banana-leaf over his shoulders by a hereditary herald of Sivaite origin entitled Sri Nara-diraja who alone outside the royal family may handle the regalia. In Negri Sembilan, at the last installation the ruler and his consort were seated on a nine-tiered bathing pavilion. Seven times the four Palace Officers circumambulated it, carrying rice-paste in a silver bowl, which each in turn presented to the royal couple, who four times dipped their right hands in it. So far from being an innovation on the Perak custom, 'in Jataka reliefs in the Ananda temple, Pagan, there are coronation anointment scenes in which Brahmans are represented as offering consecrated water in conches, in small quantities suitable for anointment'. Both in Siam and in Burma Buddhism substituted water for oil, and lustration and anointing are now apt to be merged. But in Siam after lustration the King dons royal dress and sits on a

throne, where he is handed conches of anointment water, one at each quarter of the compass as he turns about. In Negri Sembilan this part of the symbolism has been forgotten or found inconvenient to carry out and the ruler sits facing east for all four anointings, not as in Vedic ritual only for the first.

Just as in Siam Brahmins chant stanzas of benediction, so pious Malay Muslims here chant prayers for the prosperity of their ruler.

(2) After the lustration, the Perak Sultan dons royal dress. Like a Hindu god he wears a golden necklet and golden armlets, shaped like the dragon Antaboga. In his head-dress is thrust a medieval seal, whose handle, it is stressed, is made of 'thunder' (*gempita*) wood that 'causes matter to fly': it is called the 'lightning seal' (*chap halilintar*) and must have taken the place of Indra's *vajra*, or thunderbolt symbol so often represented in Javanese sculpture. In Vedic time an Indian king was given at his coronation a wooden sword termed a thunderbolt as a weapon against demons. And in Japan, where it may be only a coincidence, the Emperor after being anointed is given a wooden baton as a badge of priestly office. From the Perak Sultan's shoulder hangs a State weapon (*churika Mandakini* 'blade from the heaven-born Ganges') that still bears this name of the heavy sacrificial knife used by Aditiavarman, fourteenth-century ruler of Minangkabau, as member of a demoniacal Bhairava sect professing a Tantric doctrine that connected the worship of Siva with the worship of Buddha. This type of knife figures in the sculpture of Borobudur and Prambanan and in images of Bhairavas at Singosari (Java) and Padang Rocho (Sumatra). Aditiavarman's knife formed part of the Minangkabau regalia and was discovered as recently as 1930 in the house of an old lady descendant of the former royal family: on the obverse and reverse of the blade inlaid in gold wire are

the figures of a Bhairava and his *sakti*, one of the terrible manifestations of Siva and Mahadevi. In spite of its name the Perak weapon (unlike heavy Malay choppers called *parang churika*[1]) is a *sword* of Indian or Arab make, and in no wise archaic, though reputed to have belonged to Alexander the Great. In the Sultan's waist-belt is tucked his personal weapon, a creese. It is not on this creese but on the sword that the guardian spirits of the State may alight during the enthronement.

The ruler of Negri Sembilan whose ancestor came over from Minangkabau and carved out a throne in Malaya as late as the eighteenth century possesses no Hindu armlets and no historical state weapons. He and his consort wear handsome Malay costume and in his belt is a fine creese, a family heirloom. Thus arrayed the Malay ruler is escorted in procession round his palace grounds. The ruler of Negri Sembilan with his consort is seated under a yellow-curtained canopy on a heavy processional car, termed Maharaja 'diraja. It is not said if the car circles the royal precincts more than once but apparently not. It is drawn by a body of retainers called The Ninety-Nine. In front are carried regalia and royal umbrellas, behind the royal flags.

In Perak the Sultan circumambulates the royal demesne seven times to the thud and blare of the *naubat* drums, trumpet and clarinet, escorted by courtiers carrying flags and pennons, creeses, lances, and swords.

In modern Siam it is after the coronation that the King has circumambulated his capital the way of the sun.

This circumambulation of palaces recalls how the royal house of Sri Vijaya was connected with Mount Meru, which in Hindu and Buddhist mythology is the pivot of the universe, the heaven of Indra, wielder of the thunderbolt and controller of weather. There is no difficulty about the siting of a Mount Meru in Sumatra at Palembang—

[1] Note: Ksurika Skt., *churiga* Prakrit.

which is corroboration that the spot was a capital of Sri Vijaya. For Hinduism gave the name to many mountains just as the Olympian gods, wherever their worshippers moved, dwelt on the highest mountain there, making it an Olympus. In the museum at Batavia there is or was a sculptured Meru being transported by the gods from India to Java! So in Burma, Siam, Indochina, and Indonesia, the capitals of old kingdoms had like Angkor a hillock or like Angkor Thom a Buddhist shrine or like Bali a Hindu temple or like Mandalay a palace-tower, all of them identi- fied with Mount Meru.

> Convenne rege aver, che discernesse
> della vera cittade almen la torre.

The owner of such a hill, temple, or palace was a receptacle or incarnation of Siva or Vishnu or Indra; always of Indra where Hinayana Buddhism admitted no immortal god, the long-lived lord of Meru being the next best thing, and it was as lord of the state's symbolic Meru that the King guarded the fortunes of his people. The Tamil poem Mani- mekalai mentions two Malayan kings who claimed descent from Indra. Bhisma states that when a king is crowned, it is Indra who is crowned, and a person who desires pros- perity should worship him as Indra is worshipped. In Malay literature, the word Indra, which in Sanskrit can mean a prince as well as the god, was used to denote 'royal', as, for example, Permaisuri Indra 'royal princess' and Mahkota Indra 'royal crown'. And the synonym Isle of Indra for Penyengat where the Muslim Under-Kings of Riau lived in the eighteenth century may have had no other significance. In the same century Perak had three capitals, Brāhmana Indra, Indra Sakti, and Indra Mulia. The capital of Pahang (as also of one Sumatran State) was called Indrapura, 'the town of Indra'. The hill close behind the Negri Sembilan palace is The Hill of Sri Indra, which is unequivocal.[1] Sri Vijaya had its Sailendra dynasty, the house of the Indras or lords of the mountain.

If as in modern Siam the State religion was Hinanaya Buddhism, then the lord of the Meru might occasionally claim to be a Boddhisatva or his worldly counterpart, a Chakravartin.

To circumambulate his Meru, whether hill or palace, was for the new sovereign, Hindu or Buddhist, to take possession of his kingdom in little.

In Hindu mythology the four faces of Mt. Meru are coloured, white towards the east, yellow towards the south, black towards the west, and red towards the north. It is probably not mere coincidence that these are the colours appropriate in Perak for the Sultan, the Heir Apparent, the Prime Minister, and the Minister of War respectively.

(3) In Perak, when the Sultan has entered the palace and taken his seat on the throne, his chief herald, Sri Nara-diraja proclaims the royal title and, as a Brahmin whispers into the ear of his pupil the name of the god who is to be the child's special protector through life, so the herald whispers to his new lord the State secret, Vicitram, the name of the lord of that Meru in old Palembang, ancestor and guardian of Perak royalty. Then he reads the *chiri*, a formula in corrupt Sanskrit, extolling the new ruler as a great king 'who ravishes the three worlds by the jewels of his crown' and lauding his victory, his luck, his justice, his power of healing.

In Negri Sembilan, when the new Ruler and his consort are seated on their throne, the premier commoner chief tells the Court Herald on the Right, of the electors' choice,

[1] A Minangkabau tribal headman of Negri Sembilan, when suspected of offering a bribe to an official, protested (in 1915) that, if he were guilty, then might he be stricken by the magic of magnetic iron, by the thirty chapters of the Kuran, by the divine power of his Ruler and might his tree of life be killed by the borer-beetle of Indra Sakti!

whereupon the herald proclaims it in Brahminical attitude, that is, standing on one leg with the sole of the right foot resting against his left knee, his right hand shading his eyes and the tip of the fingers of his left hand pressed against his left cheek (p. 37 *supra*). Incense is burnt and a formula in Malay and Arabic is read, *not by one of the* 'ulama *but by one of the Four Court Officers*, an invocation to the angel of the rising sun, the angels on the right and left of the sky, the angel of the setting sun, the angel Katb of the zenith to beseech Allah to enthrone the prince; and an invocation to Karnain the horned angel of the moon[1] and to the four archangels of Islam to assist in his salvation. It was the guardians of five regions who were invoked in Vedic ritual.

It looks as if the choice of the reader of the invocation was the survival of a Brahmin privilege and as if the Herald and the Four Court Officers must once have been Brahmins just as there are still Brahmins at the courts of Siam and Cambodia. The Sri Nara-diraja in Perak was obviously of Brahmin origin, and beef is tabu for his family.

More interesting still is the fact that the combination of Perak's *chiri* with Negri Sembilan's fourfold 'anointment' and subsequent invocation to the five regions of the heavens

---

[1] The horned angel (or, in one version, princess) of the moon is an intruder. Alexander the Great was known to Muslims as Dhu'l-Karnain or 'two-horned' from a phrase in the Kuran. And Muslim missionaries, needing a pedigree for royal converts to compensate for their loss of Hindu godhead, fabricated for them descent from Alexander the champion of Islam (as their reading showed), with the genealogy of the Sassanian kings and Kaid the Indian as a link. Alexander's connection with Meru was patent! Dionysus was born from the thigh (*mĕros*) of Zeus and raiding India Alexander found near Meru the people of Nysa, named after Dionysus' nurse, who joined him in his raid on the Punjab. Once upon a time Alexander crossed to Andalus (Andalusia) and clearly this was Andalas (Sumatra); so Minangkabau folk-lore has put his tomb on the slopes of Palembang's Meru! It was therefore a brilliant thought to invoke the horned angel (or princess) of the moon to protect the descendant of Alexander the two-horned!

make up the Siamese rite when after lustration the King facing east first takes his seat on a throne. A court functionary (1) hails His Majesty as a victor and protector, and (2) offering water in a conch calls on him to guard and rule the eastern tracts of his realm. The Siamese King promises so to do and turns to the points of the compass one after the other—a similar address being made and answered at each.

Both in Negri Sembilan and in Perak the rulers have to sit as immobile as possible on their thrones, rigidity being evidence in Hindu ritual of incipient godhead. In Perak the Sultan has to remain utterly still while the *naubat* band plays a certain number of tunes, not more than nine or less than four. The Sri Nara-diraja lights the royal candles (or? candle) and asks the Sultan to fix the number of tunes. Negri Sembilan lacks the Muslim accretion of the *naubat*.

(4) The Sultan of Perak sits to hear the *naubat* enthroned, while pages bearing the regalia squat to right and left. But no account speaks of swords and daggers being displayed. In Negri Sembilan, as soon as one of the Four Palace Officers has read the invocations to the angel guardians of the five regions of the sky, the regalia are displayed, weapons being taken from their wrappings and unsheathed for a moment and then covered again. Although no mention is made of further details at the last enthronement of a ruler of Negri Sembilan, a previous record set forth how 'the Panglima Raja stands on the ruler's right and holds the Great Spear and the Panglima Sultan stands on the left and holds the Royal Sword. Beyond them are the two Laksamana similarly equipped. Beyond them are retainers with eight tufted spears, eight long creeses, eight tapers, eight water-vessels, and other symbols of power. When all is ready, the insignia are shown solemnly to the spectators. The weapons are taken out of their yellow wrappings, the royal umbrellas are opened, the royal

candles are lit, the water-vessels and betel boxes are lifted on high for all to see. A copy of the Koran is set down before these mighty regalia and ewers filled with every kind of holy water are arranged before them. One ewer contains water mingled with blood; another contains water with a bullet in it; another rice-paste.'

In Siam and Cambodia princes, courtiers, and officials drink twice a year water of allegiance in which the Court Brahmins have dipped the State Sword and other royal weapons. Newly appointed chiefs in Perak used to be sworn to allegiance on water in which the State sword had been dipped.

(5) Next, in Negri Sembilan the Herald on the Right once more assumes his uneasy Brahminical posture and calls on the four territorial chiefs to pay homage. Each chief in turn on every one of the seven steps of the dais lifts folded palms to forehead, kisses the ruler's hand three times, and still seated (cross-legged) retires backward down the steps, lifting hands in homage five times. Lesser chiefs lift hands nine times advancing and seven times retiring. In Perak, it is said, a chief touches the Sultan's knees with forehead and lips or puts his head under his Sultan's feet.

The Malay King as Caliph

(6) In Negri Sembilan the ceremony closes with a Muslim accretion, just as in Siam it closes with the modern assumption of a crown. The local Kathi recites a prayer in Malay asking Allah's guidance for the new Kalifah He has raised to the throne, the guidance He gave to the Prophet Solomon.

Here the Perak account is vague. But it is suggested that the new prayer with the Kuranic verse on Allah having appointed a new Caliph as His vicegerent precedes the homage.

So finishes the ceremony. Several kindred points deserve notice. To-day in Perak, as in Siam, the ruler's consort is separately installed, and in Perak in deference to Muslim prejudice the spectators are women. But an eighteenth-century history of Perak, the *Misa Melayu*, records how in 1756 a Sultan and his consort were enthroned together. In matriarchal Negri Sembilan in 1936 the Ruler (perhaps wrongly in theory) installed his consort first, before he was an anointed king endowed with royal authority: in Siam the King installs his consort afterwards.

There are several other parallels between Malay and Siamese kingship. As in ancient China new posthumous names are given to dead rulers. The King of Siam keeps an albino elephant, albino monkey, and albino crow: till modern times, albino children were a perquisite of the ruler of Negri Sembilan. Umbrellas must be closed near Malay as well as near Siamese palaces, as they are the homes of incarnate gods. For the same reason no one might have a higher seat than a Malay or Siamese ruler even in a carriage or car. It was taboo to spill royal blood. Head and hair of rulers were sacred. Only, however, in Trengganu has there survived a form of top-spinning conducted (several centuries ago) by Brahmins in Siam to foretell the fortunes of the realm.

In old Malacca, Perak, and Negri Sembilan there has been the same preoccupation with 4, 8, 16, and 32 that Dr. Heine-Geldern has detected in other kingdoms of Farther India and the same division into officers of the right and left hand (p. 33 *supra*). In Negri Sembilan, and probably in other States, salutes numbered 8, 16 and 32. Negri Sembilan too has 4 princes of the blood, 4 territorial chiefs, 4 major court officers, and only the ruler may have 4 wives. The regalia of the ruler of Negri Sembilan comprise 8 tufted spears, 8 swords, 8 creeses, 8 large candles, 8 small tapers, 8 betel-boxes, 8 handfuls of ashes, 8 water-vessels, 16 pennons, and 16 umbrellas. In Burma the King was required to have 4 queens, 4 lesser consorts, 4 chief ministers, 4 heralds, 4 messengers, 8 assistant secretaries. For the first part of his coronation a Siamese King sits on an octagonal throne. Fifty years ago when a shaman's *séance* was being conducted to cure him, a sick Sultan of Perak was seated on a sixteen-sided stand to await with shrouded head and grass brush in hand the advent of the spirits of the realm. There was the same kind of preoccupation with these astrological numbers in Siam and Cambodia. Generally at his enthronement a king in those countries is surrounded by eight Brahmins representing the Lokapālas who guard the eight points in the Brahmin cosmogony. Pegu in the fourteenth century had thirty-two provinces, whose governors with the King made up the number of the gods in Indra's mountain paradise. 'A passage in the New History of the T'ang Dynasty', Dr. Heine-Geldern tells us (p. 33 *supra*) refers to 'an older form of the same system, in which the provinces corresponded to constellations, the twenty-eight Houses of the Moon, and the four ministers to the guardian gods of the cardinal points. It is clear that in all these cases the empire was conceived as an image of the heavenly world of stars and gods.' On the fifth day of the Cambodian enthronement ceremonies princes and dignitaries forming a circle about the King pass round nineteen times from left to right seven disks set on tapers, whose smoke they fan towards him. This ritual symbolizes the revolution of the seven planets about Mt. Meru here represented by the king. (*JRAS*, Malayan Branch, 1947, Vol. XX.)

(References: *Sejarah Melayu*, ed. R. O. Winstedt, *JRAS. Malayan Branch*, 1938; 'History of Negri Sembilan', R. O. Winstedt, ibid., 1934; 'History of Perak', R. O. Winstedt, ibid., 1934; 'History of Malaya', ibid., 1935; 'The Installation of Tunku Abdul-Rahman as Yang di-pertuan Besar, Negri Sembilan', J. J. Sheehan, ibid., 1936; 'The Installation of Tengku Kurshiah as Tengku Ampuan', J. J. Sheehan, ibid.; 'Some Malay Studies',

APPENDIX II

R. J. Wilkinson, ibid., 1932; *Misa Melayu*, ed. R. O. Winstedt, Singapore, 1919; 'Sri Menanti', R. J. Wilkinson, *Paper on Malay Subjects*, ii, series 2, pp. 18, 19, 30, 34–44, 47; '*Adat Radja-Radja Melajoe*, Ph. v. Ronkel, Leiden, 1929; 'Conceptions of State and Kingship in South-East Asia', R. Heine-Gelden, *The Far Eastern Quarterly*, Columbia, November, 1942; *Oudheid-kundig Verslag*, Batavia, 1930; *Keris and other Malay Weapons*, G. B. Gardner, Singapore, 1936, p. 77, pl. 50, figs. 3, 4; *Siamese State Ceremonies*, H. G. Quaritch Wales; *Kingship*, A. M. Hocart; *Malay Magic*, W. W. Skeat; *The Analects of Confucius*, A. Waley, 1938, p. 236; *Pictorial History of Civilization in Java*, W. F. Stutterheim, Weltevreden, Java, figs. 54, 102, 125; *Indian Cultural Influences in Cambodia*, B. A. Chatterji, 1928, pp. 4, 5; *Indian Historical Quarterly*, 1927, vol. iii. pp. 315–355, *The Evolution of the State*, Dr. Balakrishna; *Cambodge, Fêtes Civiles et Religieuses*, A. Leclére, Paris, 1916; *The Japanese Enthronement Ceremonies*, D. C. Holtom, Tokyo, 1928.)

AUTHORITIES AND REFERENCES

The following abbreviations are used:

BEFEO = *Bulletin de l'Ecole Française d'Extrême Orient.*

EI = *The Encyclopaedia of Islam*, edited by Houtsma, London.

ERE = *Encyclopaedia of Religion and Ethics*, edited by J. Hastings, M.A., D.D. Edinburgh.

Evans = *Studies in Religion, Folk-Lore and Custom in British North Borneo and the Malay Peninsula*, by Ivor H. N. Evans, M.A. (Cambridge, 1923).

FM = *Fasciculi Malayenses*, by N. Annandale and H. C. Robinson (London, 1903).

Gimlette = *Malay Poisons and Charms*, by J. D. Gimlette, M.R.C.S., L.R.C.P. (London, 1923).

JEMSM = *Journal of the Federated Malay States Museums* (Kuala Lumpur).

JRASMB = *Journal of the Royal Asiatic Society, Malayan Branch* (Singapore, 1923–   ).

JRASSB = *Journal of the Royal Asiatic Society, Straits Branch* (Singapore, 1878–1923).

Kraemer = *Een Javaansche Primbon uit de Zestiende Eeuw*, by H. Kraemer (Leiden, 1921).

Maxwell = *In Malay Forests*, by W. G. Maxwell (Blackwood, 1907).

Montgomery = *Aramaic Incantations from Naipur*, by F. A. Montgomery, Philadelphia, 1913.

Moss = *The Life after Death in Oceania and the Malay Archipelago*, by R. Moss (Oxford, 1925).

Newbold   = *Political and Statistical Account of the British Settlements of Malacca*, by T. J. Newbold, 2 vols. (London, 1839).

Nicholson   = *Studies in Islamic Mysticism*, by R. A. Nicholson, Litt.D., LL.D. 1921.

N & Q   = *Notes & Queries*, JRASSB.

PMS   = *Papers on Malay Subjects*, First and Second Series, published by the Committee for Malay Studies, Federated Malay States, 21 vols. (Kuala Lumpur, 1907–21).

Perry   = *Megalithic Culture in Indonesia*, W. J. Perry, 1918.

S & B   = *Pagan Races of the Malay Peninsula*, by W. W. Skeat and C. O. Blagden, 2 vols. (London, 1906).

Sk   = *Malay Magic*, by W. W. Skeat (London, 1900).

SM   = *Sejarah Melayu* (or Malay Annals), 2nd edition, edited by W. G. Shellabear, 2 vols. (Singapore, 1909–10).

Thompson   = *Semitic Magic*, by R. C. Thompson (London, 1908).

Whitehead   = *The Village Gods of India*, by Rt. Rev. H. Whitehead (Calcutta, 1916).

CHAPTER I

Malaya and its History, by R. O. Winstedt (London, 1949); Whitehead, pp. 43–4; P. Mus., BEFEO, Tome 33, 1933, pp. 367–410.

CHAPTER II

ERE, vol. 11, *Shamanism*. Evans, pp. 217, 265. FM, part ii. pp. 30–3. Gimlette, pp. 18, 66. JIA, vol. I, p. 276. JRASMB, vol. I, p. 313; II, pt. III, pp. 16–19. JRASSB, No. 8, pp. 97–8, 103; No. 9, p. 107; No. 12, pp. 222–232; No. 19, pp, 100, 101; No. 29, pp. 5–7; No. 68, p. 3. Kraemer, pp. 110–123.

Maxwell, p. 303. *Misa Melayu*, ed. Winstedt (Singapore, 1919), p. 8. Newbold, ii. pp. 387–9. Nicholson, p. 121. S & B, ii. pp. 114, 226–7, 265, 308. Sk. pp. 4, 5, 41, 60–1 81–2, 581–5. Swettenham's *Malay Sketches*, pp. 153–9; Perry, pp. 141–7; Moss, *passim*; Montgomery, pp. 51–101; *Hinduism*, Monier Williams, p. 130 (London, 1878).

CHAPTER III

ERE, vol. 7, *Indonesians*, by A. C. Kruijt. Evans, pp. 268–9, 285–6. FM, part i. pp. 80, 84–6. Gimlette, p. 135. *Hikayat Awang Sulong Merah Muda*, ed. Winstedt and Sturrock, 2nd ed. (Singapore, 1914) p. 51. *The Threshold of Religion*, R. R. Marett (London, 1909). JRASMB, No. 12 (1934), pp. 172–4. *Pantun Melayu*, R. J. Wilkinson and R. O. Winstedt, Nos. 328–30, 333, 420, 695 (Singapore). JFMSM, vol. ix. parts 2 and 4, *Malay Charms*, by R. O. Winstedt. JRASSB, No. 7, pp. 23, 26; No. 9, pp. 129, 130; No. 10, p. 225; No. 16, pp. 310–20; No. 18, pp. 359–361; No. 45, p. 10; No. 49, p. 106; No. 66, p. 4; N & Q, i. p. 20, iii. pp. 74–9. S & B, ii. pp. 194, 318. Sk, pp. 151, 159, 198, 211, 216–17, 250, 355, 411, 525, 590, 609–12, 618. Thompson, p. 149; *Harvard Journal of Asiatic Studies*, vol. 8 pt. 2 (1944) 196–213.

CHAPTER IV

ERE, vol. 7, *Indonesians*; vol. 8, *Malay Archipelago*. Gimlette, pp. 21, 29, 33, 42, 72, 243. *Hikayat Anggun Che Tunggal*, ed. R. O. Winstedt (Singapore, 1914), p. 50. JFMSM, vol. ix. pt. 1, 93, pts. 2 and 4. Sk, pp. 320–1, 331, 590, 592, 599, 619, 621–2.

FM, part i. pp. 77, 101, 104; ii. pp. 21, 26, 36. JRASSB, No. 2, p. 236; No. 3, pp. 31, 97; No. 7, p. 28; No. 8, pp. 111, 129; No. 9, p. 17; No. 14, p. 309; No. 24, pp. 165–6; No. 29, p. 3; No. 32, pp. 213–4; No. 4, p. 103; No. 49, pp. 104–6; No. 72, p. 92; No. 81, pp. 11–12; No. 83, p. 133; No. 85, pp. 38–9. JRASMB, vol. III, pt. III, pp. 6–7 (1925).

Maxwell, pp. 52, 64, 121–3. Swettenham's *Malay Sketches* (London, 1900), p. 194 *seqq*.

Bijdragen tot de Taal-, Land- en Volkenkunde van Neder-landsch-Indie, xxxix. (1890), p. 102. JIA, I, p. 307. N & Q, i. pp. 40–3; iii. pp. 81–3, 126–30. Newbold, i, pp. 251–2, ii. p. 191. SM, chapter 27.

CHAPTER V

ERE, vol. 8, *Magic (Vedic)*, pp. 316, 320–1. Gimlette, *passim*. JFMSM, vol. ix. part 2, pp. 129–49; part 4, pp. 231–44. JRASSB, No. 2, p. 127; No. 7, pp. 24, 26; No. 10, p. 190; No. 45, pp. 14, 17; No. 83, pp. 88–9. Maxwell, p. 146. Skeat, pp. 11, 15, 582, 590, 592, 625, 630, 650. JIA, I. p. 308. Whitehead, *passim* P. Mus., BEFEO, Tome 33, 1933, pp. 367–410. Monier Williams, *Hinduism, passim. Malaya and its History*, R. O. Winstedt, ch. 2. PMS, *Malay Industries, Part II, Fishing, Hunting and Trapping* by R. O. Winstedt (Kuala Lumpur, 1911), p. 48. *Sacred Books of the East*, vol. xlii., M. Blomfield's *Atharva-Veda* (Oxford, 1897), p. 358.

CHAPTER VI

JIA, N.S. II, p. 129. JRASSB, No. 30, pp. 299–302; No. 31, pp. 7, 13. *Festivals and Songs of Ancient China*, by B. Granet, ed. by E. D. Edwards (London, 1932). Evans, p. 240. *Hikayat Awang Sulong Merah Muda*, p. 12. JFMSM, vol. ix. part 2, pp. 116–28. *A Dissertation on the Soil and Agriculture of the British Settlement of Penang*, by Captain James Low (Singapore, 1836). P.M.S, *Life and Customs, Part III, Malay Amusements*, by R. J. Wilkinson (1910), pp. 26–7. *Malay Industries, Part III, Rice-Planting*, by G. E. Shaw (1911), pp. 4–6, 15, 19. Sk, p. 229. India Antiqua, Leiden, 1947.

CHAPTER VII

ERE, vol. 10, *Possession*, vol. 11, *Shamanism*. Evans, pp. 158, 210–7, 271. Gimlette, pp. 69–96. G. L. Gomme's *Ethnology in Folklore* (London, 1892), p. 99. JRASSB, No. 2,

AUTHORITIES AND REFERENCES

p. 167; No. 12, pp. 222–32. Maxwell, pp. 17–24, 303. Sk, pp. 436–444. Swettenham, *ib.* pp. 153–9. JIA, vol. I, pp. 276–7; *Danses Magiques de Kelantan*, by J. Cuisinier (Paris, 1936); *A History of Perak*, by R. O. Winstedt and R. J. Wilkinson, JRASMB (1934), vol. XII, pt. I, pp. 166–171. M. Eliade, *Le Chamanisme* (Paris).

CHAPTER VIII

Ellis, *Polynesian Researches*, 2nd ed., vol. i. p. 344. Gimlette, pp. 86–91. JFMSM, vol. ix. parts 1 and 2. JRASSB, No. 16, p. 307. JRASMB (1941), vol. XIX, pt. I, pp. 131–6. N & Q, iii. p. 80. PMS, *Life and Customs, Part II, Circumstances of Malay Life*, by R. O. Winstedt (Kuala Lumpur, 1909), pp. 71–2. Sk, pp. 418–423. Westermarck's *Origin and Development of the Moral Ideas*, ii. p. 611 (London, 1908). Cuisinier, *op. cit.* Mus. P., *Cultes indiens et indigenes au Champa*, BEFEO. T. 33 (1933), pp. 367–410.

CHAPTER IX

Attar's *The Conference of the Birds*, tr. by R. P. Marani (Oxford, 1924), p. 1; L. R. Farnell, *The Attributes of God*, p. 226 (Oxford, 1925). FM, part ii, p. 35–6. Gimlette, pp. 33, 72, 78. JRASSB, No. 39, p. 39; No. 86, pp. 261–7. Kraemer, pp. 21–55, 77–123. Nicholson, p. 106 and *passim*. D. A. Rinkes' *Abdoerraoef van Singkel* (Friesland, 1909), *passim*. Sk, pp. 23, 587–8. SM, chapters 20, 32, 34. Snouck Hurgronje's 'The Achehnese', vol. ii. pp. 10–20, *Arabie en Oost-Indie* (Leyden, 1907), *passim*; PMS. *Ninety-Nine Laws of Perak*, ed. J. Rigby (Kuala Lumpur, 1908), pp. 30, 41, 48. JRASMB, vol. I, pp. 312–8; vol. III, pt. 3, p. 21; vol XV, pt. 2.

CHAPTER X

EI, sub *Abu Ma'shar, Astrology, Ja'far al-Sadik*. ERE, vol. 3, *Charms and Amulets (Muhammadan)*; vol. 4, *Divination*; vol. 8, *Magic (Indian)*. Gimlette, pp. 24–9, 47, 107, 239, 244. A. Guillaume's *The Traditions of Islam* (Oxford, 1924), p. 74. G. A. Herklot's *Zanoon-e-Islam* (London, 1832), p. 34.

Hughes' *Dictionary of Islam*, sub *Magic*. JFMSM, vol. ix. part 2; pt. 4, pp. 239, 243. JRASMB, vol. i. (1923), pp. 247, 282–300. JRASSB, No. 8, p. 147; No. 9, p. 213; No. 17, p. 155; No. 19, p. 60; No. 34, p. 32. *Mujarrabat-i-Darbi*, translated in Malay by Awang Kenali of Kelantan (lithographed A. H., 1325). N. & Q., i. pp. 23, 47; ii. p. 53. iv. pp. 124–6. PMS, *Life and Customs*, Part II, R. O. Winstedt, p. 75. *Taju'l-Mulk* ('The Crown of Kings'), Malay text by Shaikh Abbas (Egypt, A. H. 1318). *Bustanu's-Salatin*, ed. R. J. Wilkinson (Singapore, 1899). *Hikayat Iskandar Dzu'l-Karnain*, MS. Skeat, pp. 582, 591, 630, 650, 656. FM, pt. ii, pp. 37, 38. *Sha'er Ta'bir Mimpi* (lithographed, Singapore). Sk., pp. 570–3. Snouck Hurgronje's 'The Achehnese', translated by A. W. O'Sullivan (Leyden, 1906), vol. ii. p. 41. Winstedt's *Malaya*, pp. 105, 125, 129–32.

CHAPTER XI

E. Crawley's *The Mystic Rose* (London, 1920), pp. 213, 336 and *passim*. Enthoven's *The Folklore of Bombay*, pp. 150, 299. Evans, p. 227. FM, part ii. pp. 82–5. *Hikayat Awang Sulong Merah Muda*, p. 14. JFMSM, vol. ix, pt. 1, 120; vol. xv, pt. 4, pp. 180–194. JIA, I, p. 323; v, p. 610. JRASSB, No. 8, pp. 97–8, 120; No. 13, pp. 291, 294; No. 26, p. 164; No. 34, p. 34; No. 48, pp. 97–104; No. 83, pp. 90–1, 133. *Misa Melayu*, p. 40. PMS, *Life and Customs, Part I*, R. J. Wilkinson (2nd edition), pp. 1–8, 17, 18, 25–37, 55, 60; *Part II*, Winstedt, pp. 73–5, 77–86: 2nd series, *Jelebu*, by A. Caldecott, pp. 26, 52; *Johol*, by J. E. Nathan and R. O. Winstedt, pp. 13, 33–4; *Sri Menanti*, by R. J. Wilkinson, pp. 40–44. B. Schrieke: 'Some Remarks on Circumcision in Dutch India', *Tijdschrift voor Indische Taal-, Land-en Volkenkunde Deel LX, Aflevering 5 en 6*, Batavia, 1921. *The Malays* (Political Systems), R. O. Winstedt. SM, *passim*. Sk. pp. 332, 361, 364–408. Westermarck's *Marriage Ceremonies in Morocco*, pp. 101, 145, 160, 236.

INDEX

'Abdu'l-Qadir al-Jili (Jilani), 108
Abu Ma'shar (Albumasar), 89
Afterbirth, generates evil spirits, 98; formally buried, 111
Albinos, children of echo-spirit and woman, 24; perquisites of rulers, 36
Alexander the Great, Malay story of, 99
'Ali, the Caliph, 30, 58, 82, 83
Altars, magicians', 67-71
Amulets, Muslim, 92-4, 106
Ancestor-worship, relics of, 19, 20, 22, 39, 40, 43, 51, 66
Angels, Muslim, 85, 94-7
Animals, maleficent aura round dead, 21; unlucky, 91
Animism, 14-20
Aristotle, 89, 99
Astrology, 33
Asuras, 35
'Azazil, 99

Baby, rice, v. Rice
Babylon, influence of, 8, 9, 27, 31, 32, 65
Basmala, the, 93
Benua, v. Proto-Malay
Betrothal, 115-16
Birth ceremonies, prenatal, 103-5; post-natal, 106-111
Blood, soul in, 17; mixed with water for oaths, 37; white, of rajas and saints, 4
Brahma, 30, 32, 35, 58
Brahmins, Malay parallels to customs of, 16, 29, 30, 37, 108-9, 116, 122; v. Hinduism

Breath, divination from, 88; regulation of, to induce trance, 28
Buddhism, 3, 27, 36
Buffaloes, sacrificed at tribal feasts, 40
al-Buni, 93
Burial, v. death

Cats, 94; frighten spirits, 111
Charms, 94; v. Amulets, Incantations
Child-birth, spirits of women dying in, 22
China, 4, 7, 39, 65, 67, 69
Circumambulation, at circumcisions, 112; at ear-boring, 115; at weddings, 118; at installations, 37
Circumcision, of boys, 111-14; analogous ceremony for girls, 114
Combat, mock, to expel evil spirits from rice-fields, 39-40; at circumcisions, 113; at weddings, 119
Communion from feeding, 52, 65-67; of married couple, 120
Cosmogony, Malay, 29
Crocodile, avatar of Siva, 34, 82
Crystal-gazing, Malay substitute for, 89

Dancing at harvest, 53
Dead, evil spirits of, 22, v. Ancestor-worship
Death, customs at, 123-8; aerial burial, 21-2; desertion of houses at, 21-2
Demeter, 54

177

INDEX